CD INCLUDED

ESSENTIAL ROCK GUITAR TECHNIQUES

24 Skills Every Serious Player Should Master by Chad Johnson

ISBN 978-1-4584-0823-5

7777 W. BLUEMOUND RD. P.O. BOX 13819 MILWAUKEE, WI 53213

In Australia Contact:
Hal Leonard Australia Pty. Ltd.
4 Lentara Court
Cheltenham, Victoria, 3192 Australia
Email: ausadmin@halleonard.com.au

Copyright © 2012 by HAL LEONARD CORPORATION
International Copyright Secured   All Rights Reserved

No part of this publication may be reproduced in any form or by any means
without the prior written permission of the Publisher.

Visit Hal Leonard Online at
www.halleonard.com

TABLE OF CONTENTS

INTRODUCTION

Welcome to *Essential Rock Techniques for Guitar*. The aim of this book is simple: to prepare the rock guitarist with all the technical knowledge they need to tackle just about any challenge that will come their way. Though the book is organized into twenty-four technique chapters, this is a bit deceptive. For there are several technique chapters, such as Legato, Harmonics, and Tapping, that each contain numerous techniques themselves.

The techniques are laid out in alphabetical order—not in order of difficulty or frequency of occurrence. Therefore, you should think of this book as a reference. Feel free to jump to any chapter that strikes your fancy or that you need to brush up on. I do recommend working through the entire book eventually, however, as there may be ideas or concepts taught in even the most pedestrian-sounding chapters that can help shed some light in a new way. I actually learned a few things in writing this book due to similar circumstances. In doing research on certain topics, I had a few lights go off that hadn't before.

The techniques I've included here are the ones that I feel are most important and ubiquitous in rock guitar. Many of them may also be applicable to other styles, and this is an added benefit. But the main focus has been on teaching the things you need to know in order to become a competent (and hopefully exceptional) rock guitar player. I had a lot of fun writing this book, and I hope you enjoy the examples. I played them to the best of my ability, and I hope they inspire and entertain.

All the best,

Chad Johnson, 2011

THE RECORDING

Follow along with the audio icons 🔊 in the book to hear the examples on the CD. Since there are so many, most CD tracks contain multiple examples. For the particularly speedy licks, a slow demonstration is included as well at approximately half speed.

All examples (except the Whammy Bar Tricks chapter) performed by Chad Johnson

Recorded, mixed, and mastered at Tupperware Sounds Studio in Anna, TX

Whammy Bar Tricks performed by Steve Rigler and recorded at Screaming Parrot Studios in Spring, TX

ABOUT THE AUTHOR

Chad Johnson has authored over 40 instructional books for Hal Leonard, including *The Hal Leonard Acoustic Guitar Method*, *Pentatonic Scales for the Guitar: The Essential Guide*, *The Best of Nirvana Guitar Signature Licks*, *All About Bass*, *Chops Builder for Guitar*, and *Guitarist's Guide to Scales Over Chords*, to name but a few. He has toured and performed throughout the east coast in various bands and works as a session guitarist, composer, and recording engineer when not authoring or editing. He currently resides in Anna, TX (North Dallas) with his wife Allison, son Lennon, and daughter Leherie, where he keeps busy with an active freelance career.

DEDICATION

I'd like to dedicate this book to my lovely wife Allison, my beautiful son Lennon, and my little princess Leherie. I am the luckiest man in the world to have the three of you in my life.

ALTERNATE PICKING

It's fitting that, although the topics in this book are ordered alphabetically, alternate picking should appear first. It's undoubtedly one of the most important techniques to master in the world of rock guitar. As a child, you may have argued the validity of certain math subjects based on the assumption that you'd never use them in the real world. Well, consider alternate picking the "addition" of the math world; you're going to use it every single day.

With alternate picking, the concept is pretty simple: you alternate picking downstrokes and upstrokes. Generally speaking, most people prefer to pair downstrokes with downbeats and vice versa. However, the use of alternate picking, as opposed to using all downstrokes, for instance, will often depend on the tempo of the song. If you're playing eighth notes at 108 bpm, as in Example 1, alternate picking would tend to feel a bit awkward and unnecessary. This type of E blues scale riff would normally be picked with all downstrokes.

Example 1

TRACK 1
:00

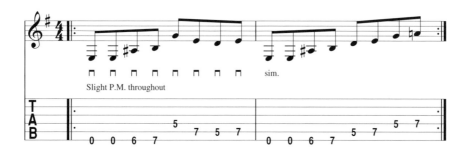

However, what if this riff was written as sixteenth notes instead? All of a sudden, consistent downstrokes would feel awkward and unnecessary (unless you're James Hetfield maybe!). And so the need for alternate picking arises!

Example 2

TRACK 1
:14

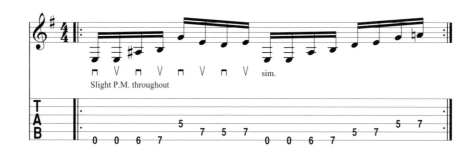

Technical Talk

While there are many books that have dedicated pages to teaching the "right way" to alternate pick, the real world just can't support the notion of only one correct method. There are simply too many examples of expert alternate pickers in numerous styles with completely different picking motions. Some pick from the wrist; others pick from the forearm. Some move just their thumb and fingers in somewhat of a circular motion. Some players angle the pick so that the front edge contacts the string first; others do just the opposite. Here's a list of several amazing pickers—each one with a distinctly different alternate picking style:

Paul Gilbert: Classic wrist motion with remaining fingers in a semi-relaxed fist shape

Steve Morse: Picks from the wrist but uses a collapsed thumb joint and hooks pinky onto high E string (or rests it on pickguard)

Eddie Van Halen: Picks from the wrist but uses mainly his thumb and *middle* finger

Zakk Wylde: Rests his remaining fingers on the pickguard and arches his wrist (when picking fast) so that he's not touching the strings at all (I don't know how he plays with so much gain without it sounding like mush!)

Michael Angelo Batio: Picks from the forearm, arches his wrist away from strings (when picking extremely fast), and tightly anchors his remaining fingers on the pickguard

Steve Vai: Picks from the wrist his with thumb joint collapsed and remaining fingers in relaxed fist

The truth is that every player's hands are different; why should one method be forced on everyone? In my opinion, the most important thing to do is to find a motion that feels natural to you and doesn't fight you and/or present other problems—i.e., you're not accidentally nudging the pickup selector on a Strat, making contact with a middle pickup, etc. Find a motion that feels relaxed and doesn't cause fatigue or pain over an extended period of time. After that, it's just a matter of practice, practice, practice.

Exercises

Synchronization

Examples 3 and 4 are designed to concentrate on two different elements: synchronization between picking and fretting hands, and moving up and down through the strings smoothly. These are perhaps the most critical elements of alternate picking. Each one of these can be moved up the fretboard as far as you like (and back down too). Also, try reversing the order of the notes as well: 4–3–2–1, 3–2–1–4, 2–1–4–3, 1–4–3–2, etc. Notice that Example 4 is the same as 3, except that we've doubled up on every note. Many people tend to think that if they can play something, picking every note only once, then picking each note twice will only be easier because the left hand only has to move half as fast. However, this is certainly not the case, as these examples demonstrate.

Example 3

TRACK 2
:00

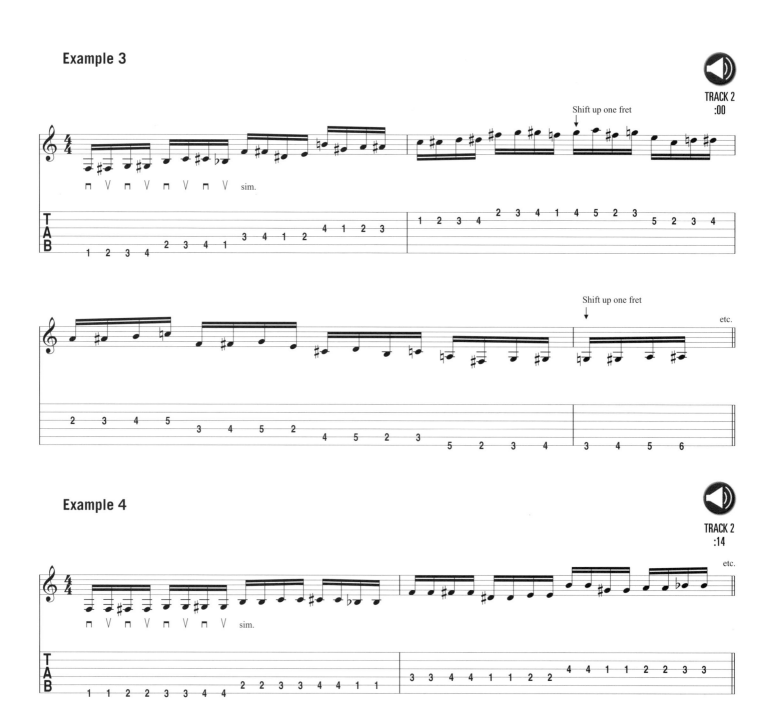

Example 4

TRACK 2
:14

Inside and Outside Picking

When moving from one string to the next, there are two different picking scenarios: *inside picking* and *outside picking*. Inside picking occurs when you stay "inside" two strings. For example, when you use a downstroke on string 2 and an upstroke on string 3, you're using inside picking.

TRACK 2
:24

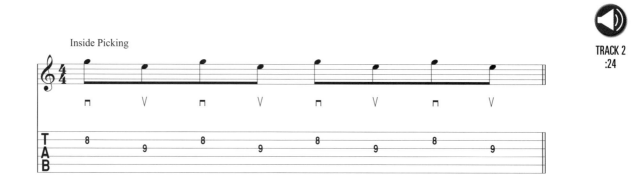

When you use a downstroke on string 3 and an upstroke on string 2, your pick travels "outside" of the string set, so you're using outside picking.

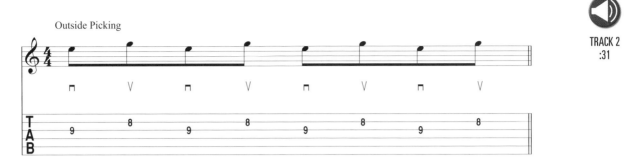

TRACK 2
:31

A great way to get plenty of practice with both types is through scale sequences. You can create sequences that will mix both types throughout or concentrate solely one type. For example, Example 5 is a typical second-position sequence in G major that mixes both inside and outside picking throughout.

Example 5

TRACK 3
:00

However, in a 3rds sequence, you can target one type only while ascending and the other type when descending. In Example 6, we ascend in 3rds through G major, using outside picking only when crossing strings. In the descending version, Example 7, we use only inside picking when crossing strings.

Example 6

TRACK 3
:26

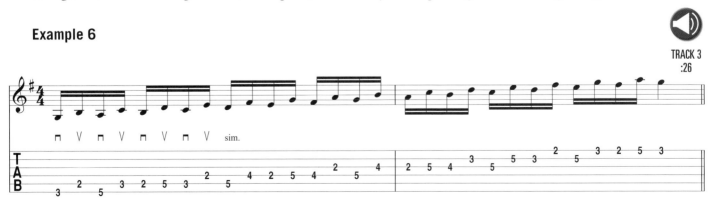

Example 7

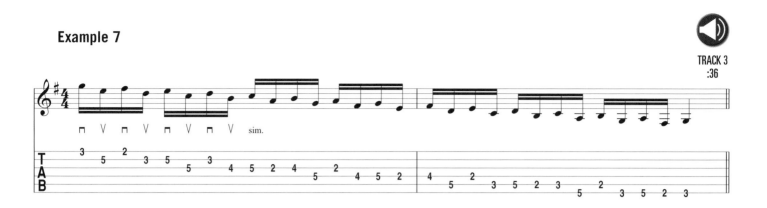

TRACK 3
:36

Three Notes Per String

Many players arrange their speedy scalar licks in three notes per string so that the picking will be consistent throughout. It's also great practice for both inside and outside picking, since alternating three notes on each string will force you to start each new string with a different pick direction than the previous. Examples 8 and 9 are typical applications in a C major scale ascending and descending, respectively.

Example 8

TRACK 4
:00

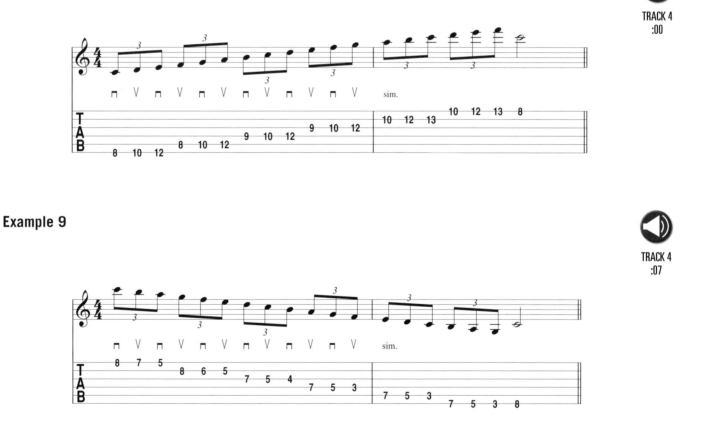

Example 9

TRACK 4
:07

Examples 10 and 11 are ascending and descending versions of a popular sequence using three-notes-per-string patterns. The ascending version will use outside picking exclusively, while the descending version will use inside picking.

Example 10

TRACK 4
:15

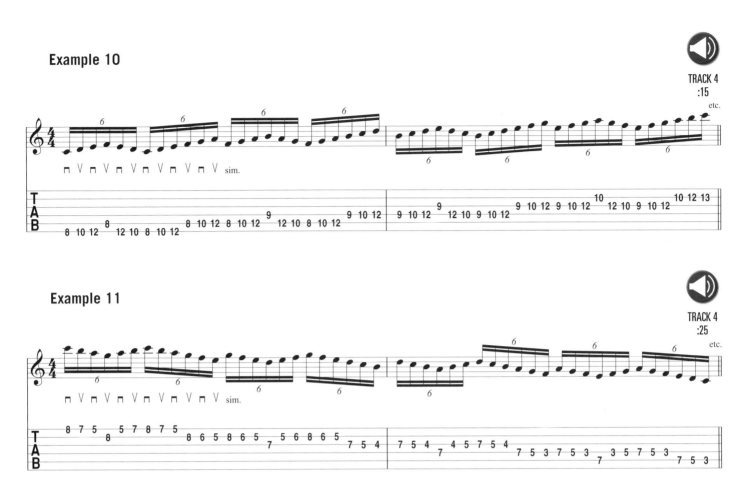

Example 11

TRACK 4
:25

Two Notes Per String

If you're a pentatonic fan, you'll use this technique quite a bit. Picking two notes per string consistently in one continuous direction will always make exclusive use of either inside or outside picking. When sequences are introduced, the other method will be employed at the beginning of each iteration. The first concept is illustrated with the ascending and descending B minor pentatonic scale run in Example 12, which uses exclusively inside picking. The latter is illustrated with the sequenced run of Example 13, which uses mostly outside picking.

Example 12

TRACK 5
:00

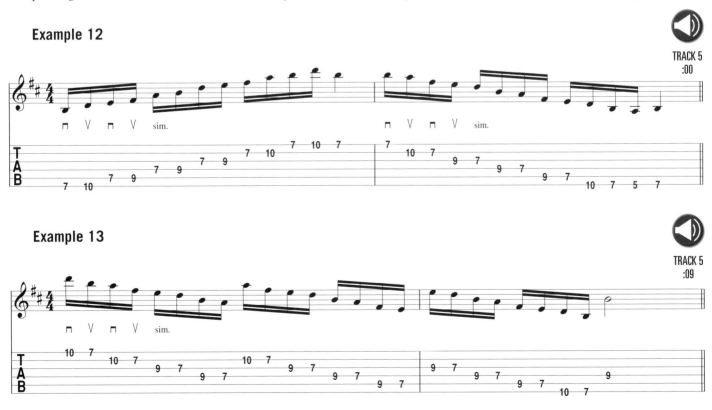

Example 13

TRACK 5
:09

One Note Per String

Less common is picking one note per string, although there are plenty of times when this will be necessary in short bursts of three or four notes. Here's a particularly demented-sounding exercise that will really help develop the loose fluidity needed to fly through notes one string at a time. Try not to let any of the notes ring together; you don't want these to sound like chords. (Most of them would be pretty ugly anyway!)

Example 14

TRACK 6
:00

And here's a nice triplet arpeggio sequence that runs up a C major arpeggio and down a D minor arpeggio. I've included a left-hand fingering so you don't have to roll the fretting hand between strings at all, which is particularly difficult to do cleanly with so many back-and-forth movements between the notes.

Example 15

TRACK 6
:13

Licks

Our first lick is in the key of E minor and uses an E Dorian mode in seventh position. It begins with some three-notes-per-string picking and moves into two-notes-per-string for the latter half. This also demonstrates an important concept that comes up in "real world" examples. It's not comprised of straight sixteenth notes; there's a pull-off and a sixteenth-note rest, both of which occupy the space of one note and should be accounted for with regards to picking direction. In other words, you're going to "skip" a downstroke in each of these instances and continue with an upstroke so that you pair downstrokes with downbeats throughout.

Example 16

TRACK 7
:00

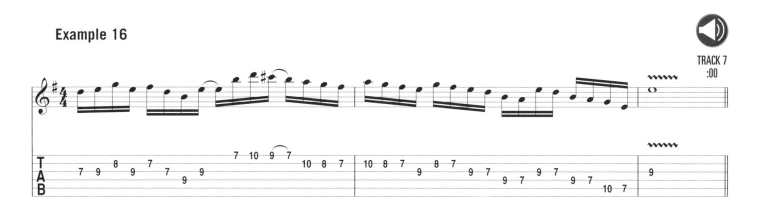

Here's one in A Mixolydian that takes place on the treble strings and begins with a sequence idea. We'll get a good mix of inside and outside picking in this one.

Example 17

TRACK 7
:23

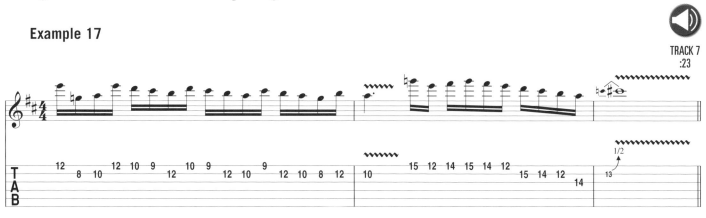

This one uses the G minor hexatonic scale (G–A–B♭–C–D–F) and makes generous use of one-note-per-string technique. It's quite angular and therefore has a bit of a fusion sound to it.

Example 18

TRACK 7
:46

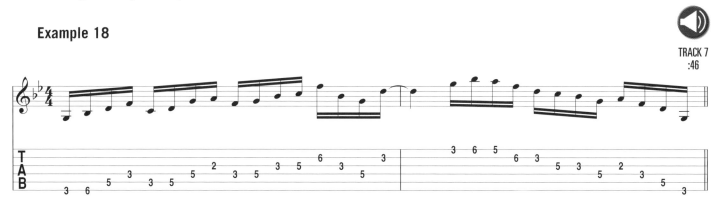

Our final lick is a three-note-per-string shred lick in B minor that uses a few sequence ideas during an ascent to a climactic bend.

Example 19

TRACK 7
1:04

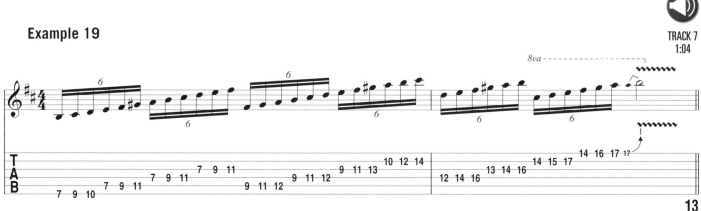

SUGGESTED LISTENING

Paul Gilbert: "Technical Difficulties" (with Racer X), "Daddy, Brother, Lover, Little Boy" (with Mr. Big)

Ozzy Osbourne: "Miracle Man"

Yngwie Malmsteen: "Black Star"

John Petrucci: "Damage Control"

BARRE CHORDS

If you want to be able to play major, minor, or seventh chords in any key, you're going to need to learn barre chords. They provide the freedom of sliding the same chord form anywhere on the neck to play a chord from any root. The tradeoff is that they're not easy for a beginner to do. It requires a specific strength in order to clamp so many strings down for an extended period of time. Fortunately, developing this strength doesn't require the time commitment of becoming an M.D. Even if barre chords are completely new to you, a few weeks of consistent practice should be all that's required.

In a barre chord, one or more fingers on the fret hand will hold down several strings at the same fret. This can technically be anywhere from two strings to all six. The important thing to remember about barre chords is that they are all generated from an open chord shape. Remember those E and A chords you learned when you first started playing? Well, those shapes are responsible for two of the most commonly used barre chord forms of all.

E-Form Barre Chords

Let's take a look at the E chord to start.

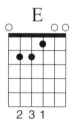

In order to transform this into an "E-form" G major barre chord, we do the following:

1) Refinger this open E chord *without* using your first finger; in other words, fret with fingers 3, 4, and 2, low to high.

2) Lay your first finger across all six strings just behind the nut. This is the E-Form barre chord shape. It's just that, in this instance, the nut is acting as your barre, which is why you don't need a finger barring all the strings.

3) Keeping this same shape, slide your hand up the neck so that your first finger is "barring" across all six strings on the third fret. And… presto! You have an E-form G major chord!

G

TRACK 8
:00

Remove your second finger, and this becomes a G minor chord. Notice how it too resembles an open E minor chord.

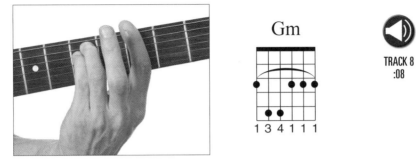

Gm

1 3 4 1 1 1

TRACK 8
:08

You can move these shapes to anywhere on the neck to play major or minor chords from any root.

A-Form Barre Chords

The other extremely common barre form is the A-form. We use the same method for it, although there are two different forms used for this chord. First, here's the common open A chord.

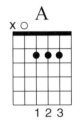

A

x o

1 2 3

In order to transform this into an "A-form" C major barre chord, we do the following:

1) Refinger this open A chord *without* using your first finger; in other words, fret with fingers 2, 3, and 4, low to high.

2) Lay your first finger across strings 1–5 just behind the nut. This is the A-form barre chord shape.

3) Keeping this same shape, slide your hand up the neck so that your first finger is "barring" across the strings on the third fret. You now have an A-form C major chord!

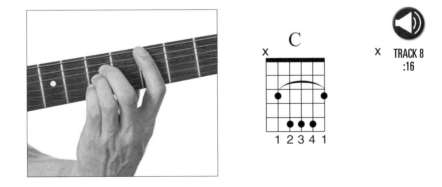

C

x   x

1 2 3 4 1

TRACK 8
:16

An alternate fingering for this involves omitting the note on the high E string. When we do that, it's common to replace the notes on strings 4, 3, and 2, which are all on the same fret, with a third-finger barre, resulting in this:

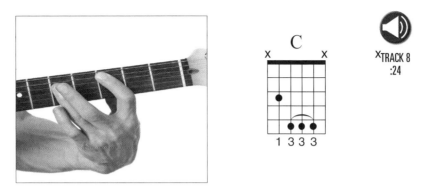

Notice that, with this form, your first finger is no longer barring; only your third finger is. Most players arch the third finger slightly so that it's touching the first string but not fretting it fully, which effectively mutes it. This allows you to strum freely without worrying about the first string sounding. (For more information on this, see the Fret-Hand Muting chapter.)

For the minor version of this chord, we revert to the first-finger barre and fret strings 4–2 with our third, fourth, and second fingers, low to high.

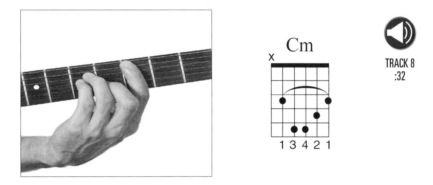

Again, notice how this exactly resembles an open Am chord.

Other Forms

There are two other barre forms that aren't used quite as often: the C-Form and the G-form. After using the same method (refingering the open forms without using the first finger), these forms are revealed as such:

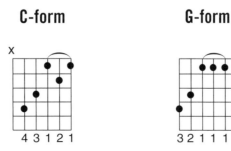

Barring with the first finger on the third fret, this results in an E♭ major C-form chord and a B♭ major G-form chord. As you can see, the G-form barre chord is quite a stretch.

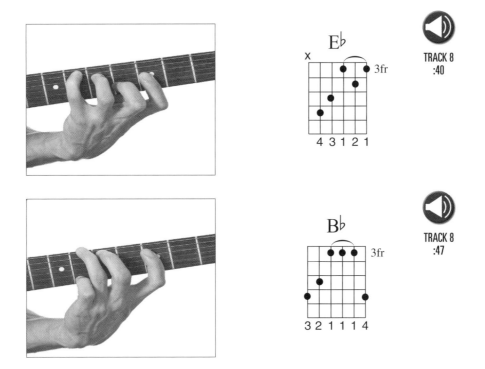

Besides the fact that these fingerings just aren't all that comfortable in the first place, another reason they're not as commonly used is that it's not possible to easily convert these into minor shapes. Try it and you'll see!

Technical Talk

With the typical E- and A-form barre chord shapes, it's important to keep your thumb behind the neck. This will make it much easier to clamp down on the strings with the pressure needed in order to maintain the barre.

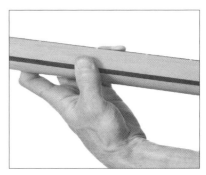

There is one exception to this: the so-called "Hendrix thumb." When playing an E-form barre chord, Hendrix would use his thumb to fret the note on the low E string. He would also usually omit the note on the fifth string (muting it by allowing the thumb to lightly touch it), resulting in this for a G major E-form barre chord:

This means that the first finger only has to barre the top two strings. It also frees up the pinky for added notes, which we'll examine later.

Some players use the thumb for the low note but keep the fifth-string note as well, like this:

Again, learning to barre just takes practice. With repetition, your fingers will strengthen, and you won't think twice about it. Just don't expect to sound great right away, because it is a specific skill. Be sure to practice plucking each note individually so that you can hear if all the notes are ringing clearly!

The Partial G-form

Although the full G-form shape doesn't see that much action, a portion of it is used quite a bit. This is the first-finger barred portion—strings 4, 3, and 2. (This could also be seen as part of the A-form shape, as these three notes are shared between these two forms, but the fact that the first finger is barring plants the hand in the G-form territory.) Here it is on the fifth fret for a C chord.

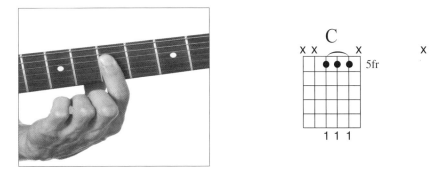

Some players will add the pinky on the sixth string (and mute the fifth string) to provide a low root note. Doing this actually enables you to convincingly fake some Keith Richards chord riffs without using open G tuning.

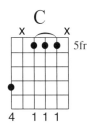

Riffs

Now let's take a look at some riffs using these barre chord shapes. The barre chord is pretty much Punk Guitar 101, and many great riffs have been crafted with nothing more. Example 1 demonstrates this with a riff in E using E- and A-form major chords.

Example 1

TRACK 9
:00

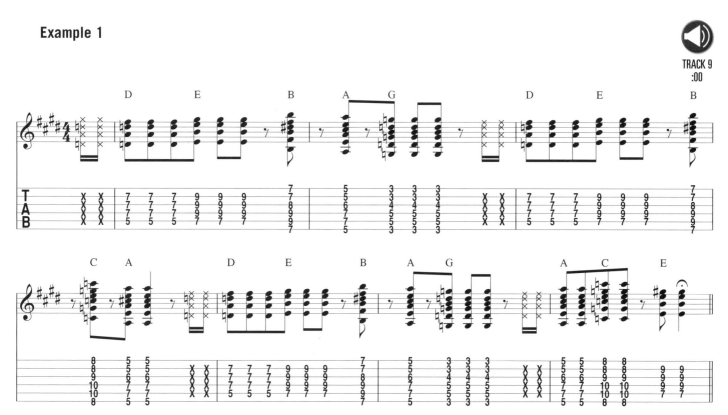

Here's another punk-style riff in G with some strategically placed rests to add some exciting syncopation.

Example 2

TRACK 9
:22

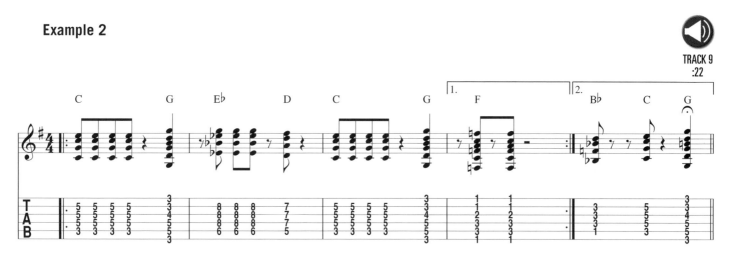

For Example 3, we're working from the partial G-form shape to create a Stones-like groove in C. Notice that some of the embellishments we're using could be seen as a "partial C-form." The first finger is anchored on the fifth-fret barre for most of the riff. For the final chord, we add the pinky on the top string for the high C note. This is another common addition on the partial G-form shape.

Example 3

TRACK 9
:39

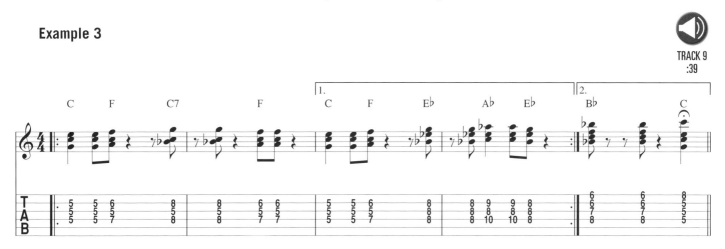

Example 4 demonstrates the Hendrix thumb technique with a riff in A. In typical Hendrix fashion, we're embellishing the chords with lots of hammer-ons and slides. Notice how the A-form and G-form chords are bridged for the D chord in measure 2.

Example 4

TRACK 9
:59

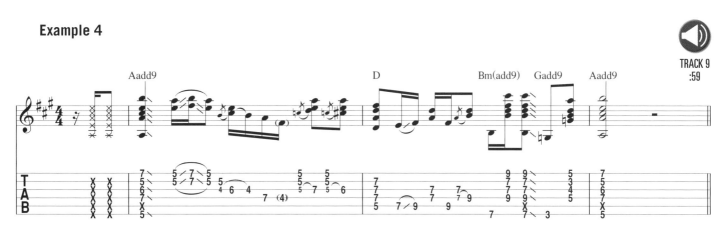

SUGGESTED LISTENING

Jimi Hendrix: "Castles Made of Sand," "Bold as Love"

The Kinks: "You Really Got Me"

Red Hot Chili Peppers: "Under the Bridge"

Sublime: "Santeria"

BENDING

String bending is one of the most expressive tools on the guitar. It allows us to simulate the scooped notes of vocalists—most notably in a blues style—and it can also add excitement and tension to our phrases. We can use bends to nail "in the cracks" notes that lie between two distinct pitches, or we can make them very precise and mimic the sound of a pedal steel guitar or a pitch wheel on a synthesizer.

Often, bending to a note instead of playing the fretted equivalent can lend an entirely different character to a phrase. Sometimes, the difference is so profound that a phrase played without a bend is almost unrecognizable. For example, take this phrase in the key of A, which is not commonly played on the guitar.

Example 1

TRACK 10
:00

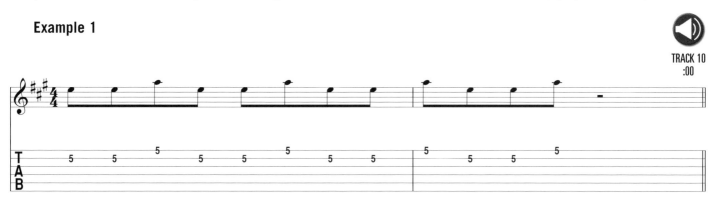

When we replace the first E note with a D bent to E, however, we have one of the most classic guitar licks in rock history.

Example 2

TRACK 10
:08

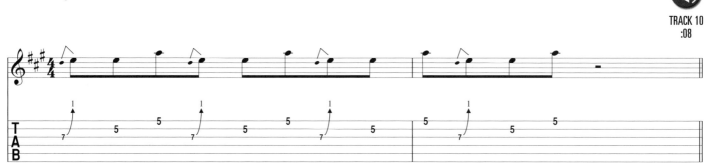

Technical Talk

Bending (or stretching) a guitar string raises the pitch. The farther you bend, the higher the pitch is raised. Like barre chords, this is a specific type of muscle development that will take a bit of time to work up. With practice though, this will pass, and you'll be bending all over the neck without a single wince. You'll find that the closer you are to the twelfth fret, the easier it is to bend. Bends on frets 1–3 are extremely difficult and will require serious finger strength.

In the music, the distance of the bend is described in *steps*. On the guitar, a half step is the distance of one fret on a string. A whole step (also "full step" or just "step") is the distance of two frets, and so on. Wider bends of 1 1/2 steps, two steps, or more are not unheard of either. We also make frequent use of *microtonal* bends—i.e., bends smaller than a half step. The quarter-step bend is half the distance of a half-step bend. This is extremely useful in bluesy styles.

Generally speaking, for bends on strings 1–3, which are the most common, the strings are "pushed" up toward the ceiling (or toward the sky if you're communing with nature), while bends on strings 4–6 are "pulled" down toward the floor. There are exceptions to this rule, but it's certainly a good place to start. The reasoning is quite simple. You can't pull down very far—and therefore raise the pitch—on string 1 before you run out of fretboard!

Supporting the Bending Finger

All four fingers can be used to bend, but the most commonly used by most players is the third finger. This is a bit deceptive, however, because it's rare that any finger bends alone. Usually, when bending a string with the third finger, the first and second fingers help out "behind the scenes" by pushing up as well. This makes maintaining a constant pitch much easier and also aids in keeping unwanted noises from popping out (see the Fret Hand Muting chapter).

Bending with third finger
with support from first
and second

When bending with other fingers, the same concept applies. The remaining fingers help out behind the bending finger.

Bending with fourth finger
with support from first,
second, and third

Basically, the only finger that does bend alone is the first finger. Because of this, it's probably the least used in terms of large bends of a full step or more. (It is used all the time for quarter-step and half-step bends though.)

Bending with second finger
with support from first

Bending with first finger

Exercises

Let's work on the technique with a few exercises. With any bending lick in general, it's highly recommended to check the pitch of your bend by playing the target pitch as a fretted, unbent note. We'll be doing just that in each of these exercises.

Basic Bends

In this first example, we're going to bend string 3 up a whole step. This is likely the most common bend on the guitar. Listen very closely to the pitch of the unbent note and make sure you're matching that with your bend. Try it first with your third finger as the bending finger (supported behind with the others). Then try it with each other finger.

Example 3

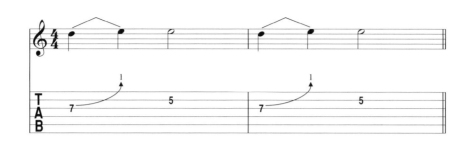

TRACK 11
:00

Now let's try the same thing but with a half-step bend. Again, be sure to try the bend with each finger.

Example 4

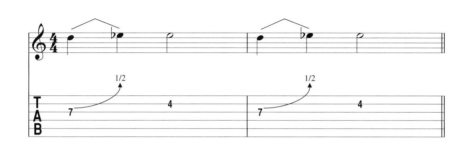

TRACK 11
:11

In Example 5, we'll follow the same process on strings 2 and 1. Notice that, when bending on string 1, we need to move out of position in order to hit the unbent target note. Take your time with this. We're just checking the accuracy of the bend.

Example 5

TRACK 11
:21

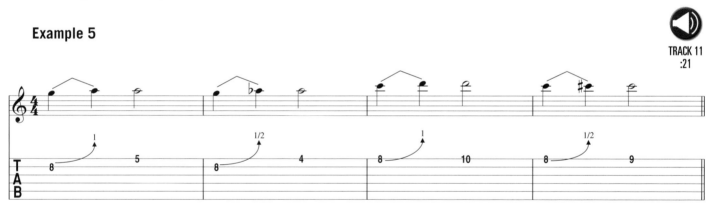

In Example 6, we'll use the same procedure with bends on the bottom three strings. For these bends, pull the strings down toward the floor. Be sure to try it with all four fingers.

Example 6

TRACK 11
:36

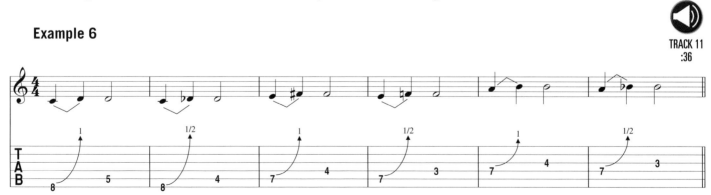

Grace-Note Bends

With a *grace-note bend*, we're bending up to the target pitch immediately. This will require a good sense of muscle memory because you won't hear the pitch slowly rising. You need to memorize the distance required to hit the pitch. For this first exercise, we'll work through the strings with whole-step bends. Remember to support the bending finger!

Example 7

TRACK 12
:00

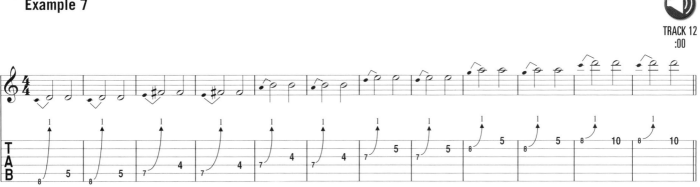

And now we'll try half-step grace bends. Be sure to bend with each finger!

Example 8

TRACK 12
:36

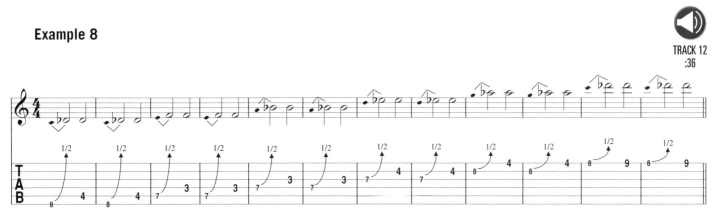

Pre Bends

With a *pre bend*, you'll be bending the string before you even pluck it. This means you'll really need to have those bends down cold! Go back and forth with the pre-bent note and the unbent target pitch to make sure you're accurate. Let's start with some whole-step pre bends.

Example 9

TRACK 13
:00

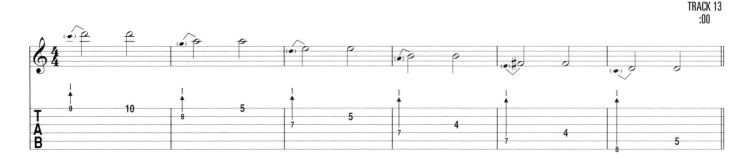

And now let's try some half-step pre bends.

Example 10

TRACK 13
:21

Licks

Now that you've got a grip on the basic technique, let's put it to use with some classic bending licks. This first one in A uses a quarter-step bend on the first string. Notice that it's not quite a half step; it gives it a bluesy touch.

Example 11

TRACK 14
:00

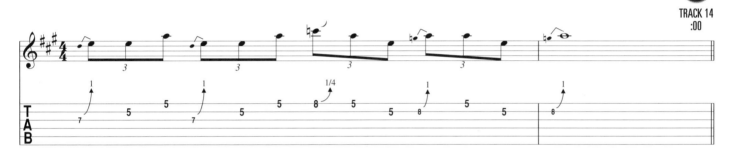

Here's one in the key of C minor that uses several quarter-step bends.

Example 12

TRACK 14
:09

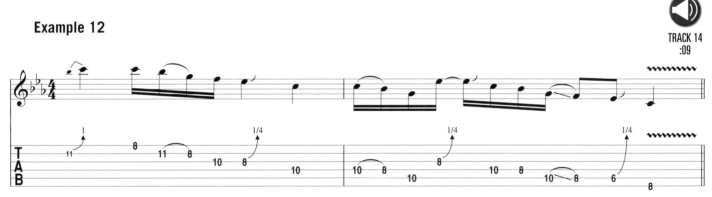

This one in the key of D uses a few pre bends and ends with a half-step bend to hit the major 3rd, F#.

Example 13

TRACK 14
:20

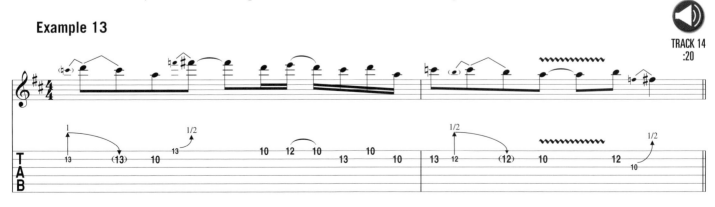

In this lick in B minor, we're using another common whole-step bend in the pentatonic extension box before moving back into the standard box.

Example 14

TRACK 14
:31

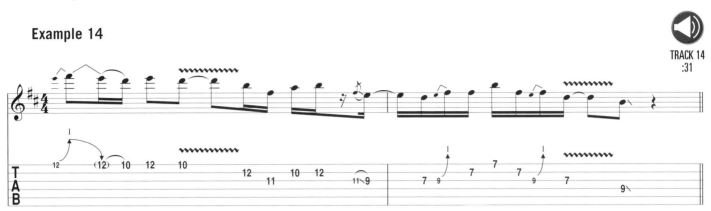

Advanced Bending Concepts

Now let's check out a few more licks that make use of some advanced bends. This first one uses what's called an *oblique bend*. It's basically a double stop in which one string is bent and the other remains stationary.

The technique is ubiquitous in Southern rock, but it's also common in blues, metal, and many other genres. Let's check it out with a country rock lick in G. I prefer to hold the fifteenth fret with my pinky and bend with the third finger (supported, of course!), but some will hold the top note with their third finger and bend with the second. See which way feels best to you.

Example 15

TRACK 15
:00

And here's another take on an oblique bend in D minor. We're bending the second string this time and holding a note on the first. Again, experiment with the fingering to see what feels best to you. I use the ring/pinky combination on this one as well.

Example 16

TRACK 15
:10

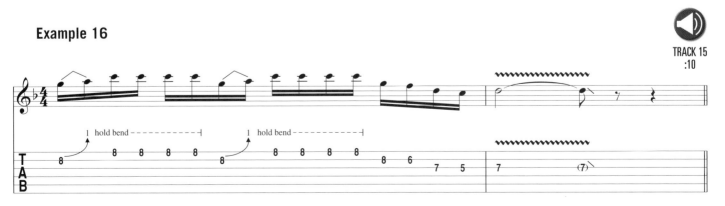

Also common are *double-stop bends*, in which you're bending two notes (usually on adjacent strings) at the same time. Some players prefer to use the same finger to bend both strings, while others like to fret the notes with two different fingers.

Try it out on this gritty lick in C.

Example 17

TRACK 15
:19

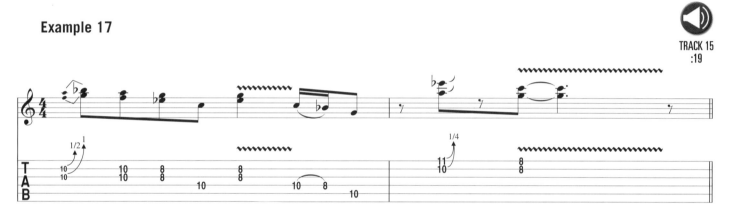

And here's one in A that works some bends on the lower strings, though it also includes a double-stop bend and release.

Example 18

TRACK 15
:29

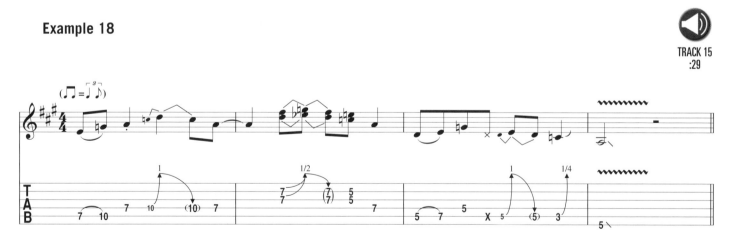

Our final advanced bending concept we'll look at is the *unison bend*. With this concept, you're sounding the bent note and the target unbent note at the same time. It's a great, gritty sound that's very common as well. Here's a lick in E that uses two different unison bends.

Example 19

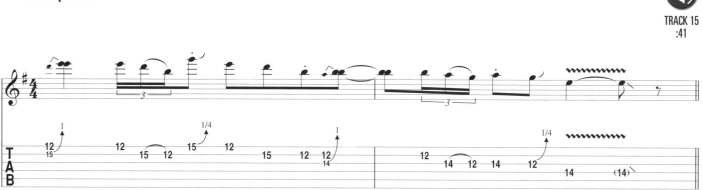

SUGGESTED LISTENING

Led Zeppelin: "Heartbreaker," "Whole Lotta Love"

Stevie Ray Vaughan: "Tightrope"

Jimi Hendrix: "Machine Gun"

Lynyrd Skynyrd: "Gimme Three Steps," "Freebird"

Santana: "Black Magic Woman"

DOUBLE STOPS

A *double stop* is created when you play two notes at once. Though this is most commonly done with notes on adjacent strings, non-adjacent strings are used as well. They're used in all forms of rock, blues, country, and many other styles. Aside from adding extra intensity to a solo phrase, they've also helped to create some classic, timeless riffs.

The musical term for the distance between two notes is the *interval*. All double stops are comprised of a certain interval. There are several intervals commonly played as double stops on the guitar, but the most common are 3rds, 4ths, 5ths, and 6ths. It's beyond the scope of this book to thoroughly explain the concept of intervals, but here are some basic qualities of intervals that apply universally.

- There are five interval *qualities*: major, minor, augmented, diminished, and perfect

- 2nds, 3rds, 6ths, and 7ths are normally major or minor

- 4ths and 5ths are normally perfect or augmented; 5ths can also be diminished, and 4ths can also be augmented

- A major interval is one half step larger than a minor interval—i.e., a major 2nd is one half step larger than a minor 2nd

- A diminished interval is one half step smaller than a perfect interval—i.e., a diminished 5th is one half step smaller than a perfect 5th

- An augmented interval is one half step larger than a perfect interval—i.e., an augmented 4th is one half step larger than a perfect 4th

There's more to it than that, but you'll be ok for now with the above information.

Technical Talk

On the guitar, these double stop intervals create shapes that are easily memorized. Here are the shapes for the most common double stops on each set of adjacent strings.

Minor 3rds

Major 3rds

Perfect 4ths

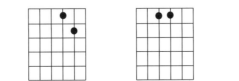

Diminished 5ths (Also known as Augmented 4th)

Perfect 5ths

Minor 6ths

Major 6ths

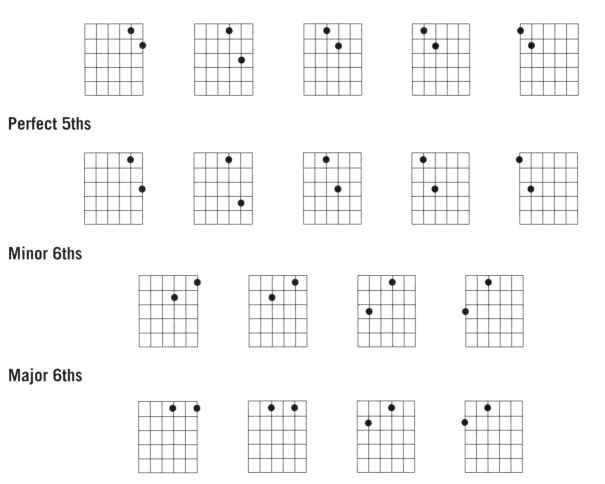

Note that, although 5ths were shown here on adjacent strings and 6ths were shown on non-adjacent strings, they are occasionally played the other way. Here are those alternate shapes.

Perfect 5ths (Non-adjacent Strings)

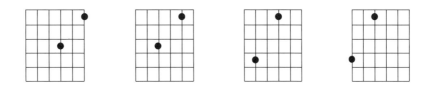

Minor 6ths (Adjacent Strings)

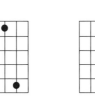

Major 6ths (Adjacent Strings)

Pick Hand Options

With double stops, you have several options with regards to plucking. You can either use the pick to strike both notes, use *hybrid picking* (the pick and a finger), or use fingers only. Hybrid picking or fingerstyle will result in a more piano-like attack, with both notes sounded precisely at the same time. Using the pick only presents an additional concern when you're playing non-adjacent double stops. You'll need to mute the in-between string with your fret hand fingers to prevent it from ringing out. (For more information on this, see the Fret-Hand Muting chapter.)

Exercises

Harmonizing a scale with double stops is an excellent way to become familiar with the different shapes. It's a fairly easy process, and there are numerous variations you can employ to get some great practice with double stops of all shapes and sizes.

Let's start by moving laterally along the neck and staying on the same string set. In Example 1, we'll play through one octave of a C major scale in 3rds, remaining on strings 1 and 2 throughout.

Example 1

TRACK 16
:00

Now let's try the same thing on strings 2 and 3. When we reach the twelfth fret, we'll shift down an octave to the open strings.

Example 2

TRACK 16
:17

We can do the same thing on the remaining string groups.

Example 3

TRACK 16
:31

Example 4

TRACK 16
:46

Example 5

TRACK 16
1:02

Another good exercise is to work vertically across the neck. Here's the same C major scale in 3rds, but we're ascending two octaves this time. We remain between frets 7 and 12 the entire time (except for the very last one!).

Example 6

TRACK 16
1:17

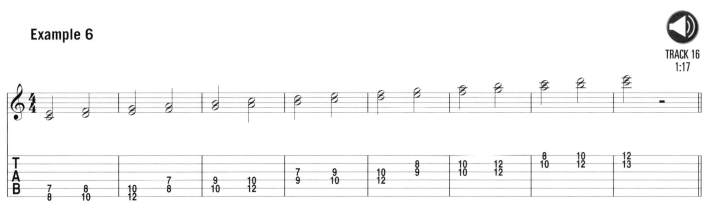

Working laterally along the neck in 6ths is also very common. Here's the one-octave C major harmonized scale in 6ths on each non-adjacent string group.

Example 7

TRACK 17
:00

Example 8

TRACK 17
:16

Example 9

TRACK 17
:32

Example 10

TRACK 17
:47

And now let's work through the scale in 6ths vertically across the neck, remaining between frets 7 and 12.

Example 11

TRACK 17
1:03

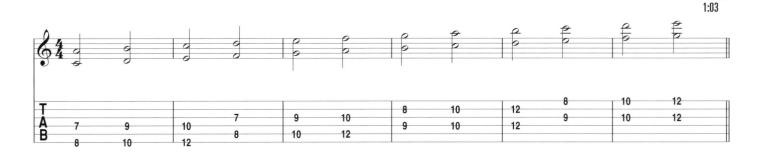

Harmonizing the scale vertically with 4ths and 5ths is useful as well. Watch out though, because they're not all perfect intervals. You'll have one augmented 4th in Example 12 and one diminished 5th in Example 13. Notice also that we're mixing adjacent and non-adjacent string groups for the 5ths example so that we remain in one area on the fretboard.

Example 12

TRACK 17
1:23

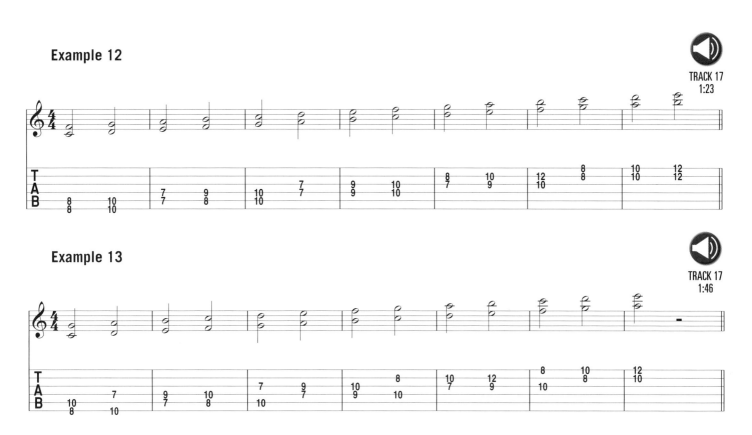

Example 13

TRACK 17
1:46

Licks

Now let's check out some double-stop licks. This first one is in D and shouldn't be too much trouble after those exercises. We're playing 3rds in D Mixolydian (same notes as a G major scale) on two different string groups.

Example 14

TRACK 18
:00

In this B minor lick, we're playing 4ths from the B minor pentatonic scale. This is another common approach—one employed by Ritchie Blackmore for a certain "smoky" riff.

Example 15

TRACK 18
:11

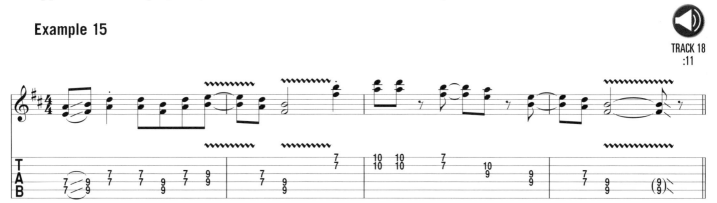

Here's one in G that's got a soul flair to it. We're using 6ths similar to the way Steve Cropper would.

Example 16

TRACK 18
:26

Hendrix loved his double stops, so we can't quit without something in the style of him. However, he added all kinds of color to his double-stop lines by incorporating hammer-ons, slides, and pull-offs—something he actually picked up from soul guitarists such as Steve Cropper and Curtis Mayfield. In this lick in C, we're mixing mainly 4ths and 3rds, but we're embellishing them with all the above-mentioned techniques the way Hendrix often would.

Example 17

TRACK 19
:00

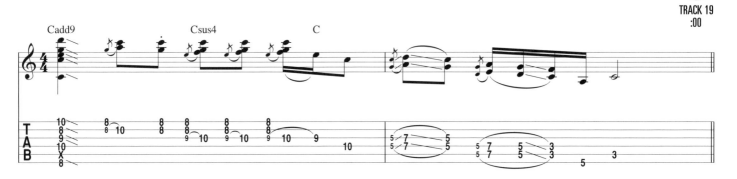

Another favorite move of Hendrix, which has also been adopted by Eric Johnson, is sliding non-adjacent 5ths. This is often done by traversing a minor pentatonic scale on string 4 while harmonizing a 5th above on string 2. Here's a typical application in A minor. Remember to mute string 3 (unless you intentionally want it to ring out).

Example 18

TRACK 19
:16

Another master of the double stop was Chuck Berry. This final lick in C demonstrates some classic Berry licks of this type.

Example 19

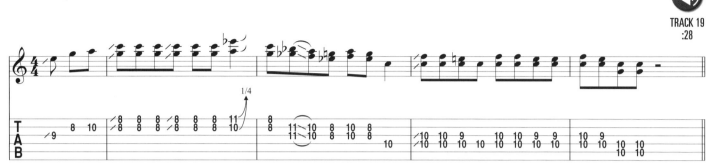

SUGGESTED LISTENING

Jimi Hendrix: "Bold as Love," "Little Wing"

Chuck Berry: "Johnny B. Goode"

Deep Purple: "Smoke on the Water"

Van Halen: "Beautiful Girls," "5150"

Steve Vai: "Viv Woman," "Goin' Crazy!" (with David Lee Roth)

ECONOMY PICKING

This technique may have a funny name, but some players seriously swear by it. In fact, many players get in outright debates about which method is superior: alternate picking or economy picking. The truth is, there doesn't need to be a debate, and one method doesn't need to be awarded a blue ribbon. Many players actually make use of both methods with great success.

The concept in alternate picking is simple: you alternate picking downstrokes and upstrokes. The concept in economy picking is simple as well, but it's a different way of thinking. It has to do with how you approach the idea of crossing to the next string. The bottom line is this: with economy picking, you continue the same picking direction whenever possible when moving to an adjacent string.

For example, instead of picking this triplet phrase with alternate picking, you would pick it as shown: down-up-down, down-up-down, etc.

Example 1

TRACK 20
:00

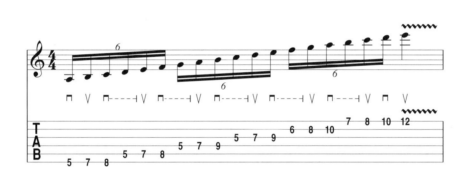

Technical Talk

Some players gravitate toward this technique on their own from the very beginning, but that seems to be the exception. Most players, especially ones that take any formal lessons, begin with alternate picking. And if you're used to alternate picking, economy picking will feel very strange at first. You'll need to almost unlearn some engrained habits, and it really can feel as if you're starting from scratch in the pick hand. Learning economy picking won't hurt your alternate picking technique though (and vice versa), and there are several examples of shred monsters that make use of both techniques with jaw-dropping results—namely Yngwie Malmsteen and Michael Angelo Batio. The sound is usually smoother than alternate picking as well—something that you may or may not want for a particular phrase. It's nice to have the option of either technique available for this reason.

The main thing to remember is that, when crossing strings, you want to drag your pick across the two strings with one motion. This is why picking directions like down-up-down, down-up-down can be deceiving. It's not really two downstrokes in a row; it's more like one continuous stroke. (This is why, in Example 1, the picking indications were drawn as they were.) After picking the third note on the sixth string in Example 1, for instance, allow your pick to move on to string 5 without stopping and pick it. With regards to the actual motion of the pick hand, most economy pickers use a combination of wrist and forearm motion. The wrist motion usually occurs when picking on a single string, whereas the forearm movement usually occurs as you "drag" or "slide" the hand over in position when crossing strings.

Without a doubt, one of the indisputable masters of the economy picking technique is fusion guitarist Frank Gambale. If you're serious about developing the technique, you'd do well to check out his instructional videos, as he spends considerable time demonstrating the ins and outs of economy picking in great detail.

Exercises

Three Notes Per String

Economy picking lends itself extremely well to three-notes-per-string patterns, and once the technique is mastered, you can fly through scales at a blinding pace with very little pick-hand movement. Let's start with a few ascending and descending scales using three notes per string.

Example 2

TRACK 20
:08

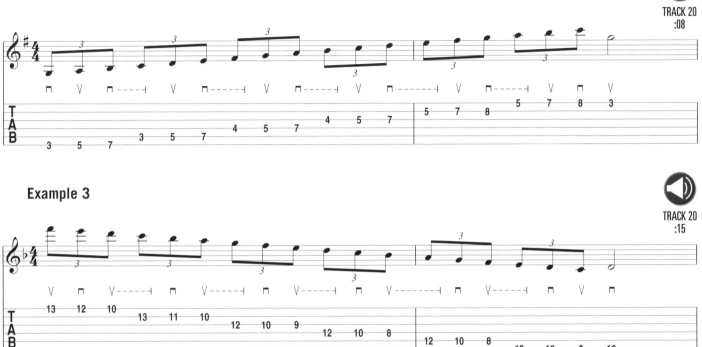

Example 3

TRACK 20
:15

Alternating Three Notes and One Note

The typical pentatonic box shape is impossible to play with economy picking. However, with a bit of left-hand stretching, we can arrange the notes on the strings in a 3-1-3-1-3-1 pattern that makes economy picking possible. This means that you'll be picking across three strings with one continuous stroke, which will take a bit of getting used to.

Example 4

TRACK 21
:00

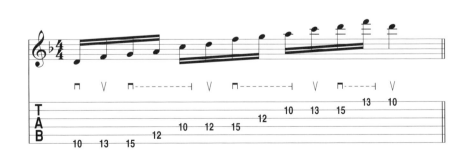

Example 5

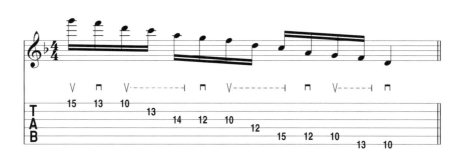

TRACK 21
:07

Moving Up or Down the Neck with Two Notes Per String

Another interesting application of economy picking is moving four-note fragments arranged as two notes per string up or down the neck. This is often done with the pentatonic scale. It's a very interesting motion and one that's a lot of fun once mastered.

Example 6

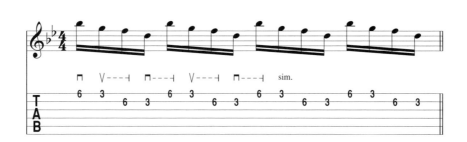

TRACK 21
:12

Example 7

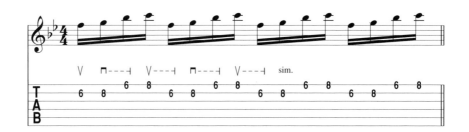

TRACK 21
:18

Triad Arpeggios

Another common application for the technique is triad arpeggios arranged on two strings. Yngwie is a master at this type of thing. Notice that this isn't true economy picking; if it were, we'd continue back with another upstroke on the fourth note. Therefore, we can think of this as more of an economy/alternate hybrid technique.

Example 8

TRACK 21
:24

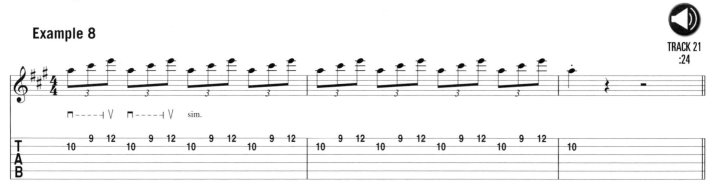

Example 9

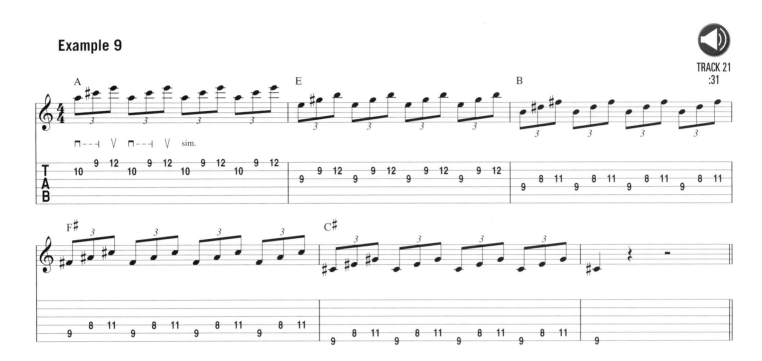

Licks

Now on to the licks. This first one ascends through a three-notes-per-string pattern in C minor and finishes off with a quick descent to string 2 before capping it off with a final bend.

Example 10

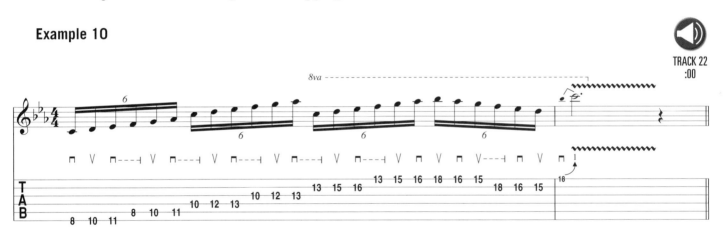

Here's an ascending phrase that works its way up the neck in D minor on strings 3 and 4 throughout. Make sure the timing is even throughout; it's easy to rush certain notes on licks like this one.

Example 11

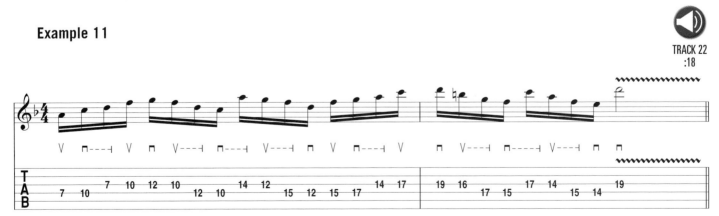

In this C Dorian lick, we're mixing in some two-string mini-sweeps (see the Sweep Picking chapter) along with some scalar playing. Learn this one slowly first; there are a lot of specific picking problems to be worked out.

Example 12

TRACK 22
:32

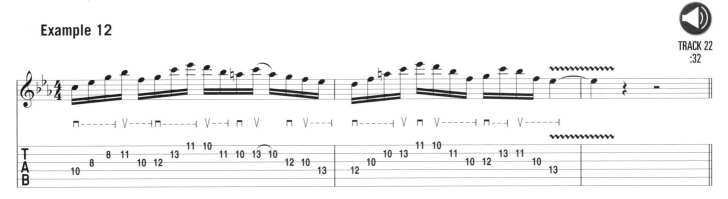

Here's a triad workout on strings 2 and 1, Yngwie-style. Good luck getting it up to his speed!

Example 13

TRACK 22
:51

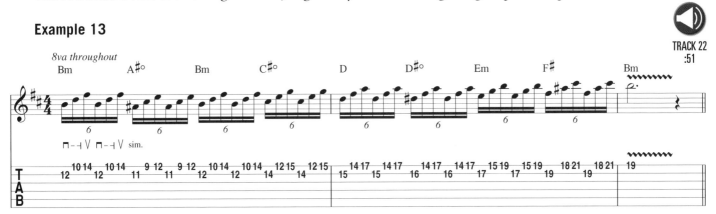

This final lick has a bit of a fusion sound to it, in the vein of Frank Gambale or Allan Holdsworth. There are some stretches in the fret hand that can be problematic, so take it slowly and make sure all the notes are speaking.

Example 14

TRACK 22
1:15

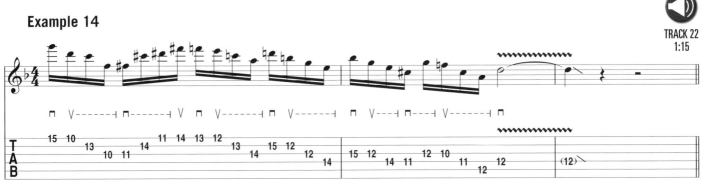

SUGGESTED LISTENING

Yngwie Malmsteen: "Rising Force"

Frank Gambale: "Duet Tuet," "Frankly Speaking"

Michael Angelo Batio: "Speed Kills"

George Bellas: "The Dawn of Time"

FRET-HAND MUTING

Fret-hand muting is a thankless job. Think of it like a sound man; everyone expects their work to be perfect, and the only time you hear comments about them is when something goes wrong. Fret-hand muting is the same way. It's the behind-the-scenes technique that makes all the other flashy techniques like legato, bending, tapping, and slide guitar sound so good. Though it's rarely talked about, it's an absolutely integral part of blues and rock technique.

The purpose of fret-hand muting is basically to keep unwanted noises out of your licks or riffs. However, this is a bit of a limited definition, as it's also employed for the purpose of adding *wanted* noises to your riffs. Think of that big, fat boogie pattern Stevie Ray plays at the beginning of "Pride and Joy" when the band enters. That sound is not possible without a solid fret-hand muting technique.

Technical Talk

In order to discuss fret-hand muting, we need to get out of the mindset that there's only one correct technique for all guitar playing. Yes, classical guitar teachers cringe when they see the thumb creep over the top of the neck. But rock guitar is *not* classical guitar. Just as the classical technique (thumb behind the neck, fingers arched, etc.) suits that style, rock technique (thumb sometimes over the neck, fingers laid more flat, etc.) is designed for rock guitar.

Let's say you're playing this G note here on fret 5, string 4 with your first finger.

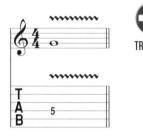

TRACK 23
:00

(referenced again at the bottom of this page)

A classical guitarist would fret the note this way, with the finger arched and the thumb centered on the back of the neck.

However, a rock guitarist may fret the same note this way, with the first finger laying flatter and the thumb hanging over the top of the neck.

Why? Because a rock or blues guitarist may be really laying into the note with an extremely heavy pick attack and applying intense vibrato. Even though the note is on the fourth string, he may be picking through *all six strings* to give the note added weight and punch. (This is exactly what Stevie Ray is doing in the "Pride & Joy" reference.) When this is done, you'd better be muting all but the string you want to sound, or you'll be in for a noisy, nasty surprise. In the photo, you can see that the thumb is lightly touching the sixth string to keep it quiet. Along with fretting the G note, the tip of the index finger is lightly touching the fifth string to keep it quiet. And the third, second, and first strings are kept quiet by the underside of the first finger.

This is not to say that rock guitarists always use this technique for every note they play—far from it. But it happens often enough, and many players instinctively develop this coordination in order to mimic the sounds they hear other players make. Funky styles make use of it all the time, as do bluesier rock styles. To demonstrate, let's now listen to that G note played both ways: first by picking only the fourth string, and then by muting with the fret hand so that we can pick through all six strings for added punch.

It makes quite a difference, as you can hear. Of course, not all players do this, and there are some rock players that lean more toward the classical technique side. But there are plenty of common, specific instances when it's absolutely necessary. Let's take a look a few of those.

Strumming Octaves or Other Intervals on Non-Adjacent Strings

Strumming octaves is a fairly common practice in rock guitar. It creates a big sound and is perfect for strengthening a melody that needs to be bold and brash. However, there's simply no way to do this without enlisting the help of the fret hand for muting purposes. Let's look at this D octave shape on strings 5 and 3 as an example.

Notice the following in the photo:

- The tip of the first finger is muting the sixth string

- The underside of the first finger is muting the fourth string (the tip of the third finger may also aid in this)

- The underside of the first finger lays flat to mute the treble strings as well

With this technique, you're allowed to strum freely through all six strings without worrying about anything coming out except the octave notes. When playing octaves on strings 4 and 2 or strings 3 and 1, however, an extra muting component is necessary. Let's look at this G octave shape.

Notice that the first finger is continuing to mute the adjacent lower (fifth) string as well as the middle string (third) between the octave notes and the higher strings (first). However, the second finger also now comes into play to mute the sixth string by lightly touching it. When playing octaves on strings 1 and 3, the second finger would mute both the fifth and sixth strings.

Let's hear how this solid muting technique allows for a clear statement of an octave melody with no worries of extraneous noises.

Example 1

TRACK 23
:14

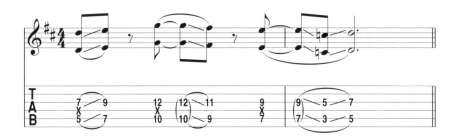

The same goes for other intervals on non-adjacent strings, such as 6ths and 5ths. When playing this major 6th shape on strings 4 and 2, for example, the use of fingers 3 and 4 (low to high) allows your first and second fingers to easily mute all the other strings behind.

For this 5th shape on strings 4 and 2, things are a bit trickier, because you don't have the first finger to help much with muting.

The tip of the third (or second) finger can keep the fifth string quiet, but we'd really like to mute the sixth string as well so we don't have to worry about avoiding it when strumming rigorously. So we have two options:

1) Use the thumb to mute the sixth string.

2) Bring the second finger over to mute the low E string (it can also help to mute the fifth as well).

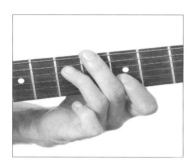

Let's hear how this sounds with a riff that makes use of both 6ths and 5ths.

TRACK 23
:23

Example 2

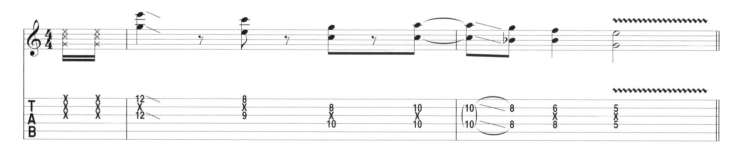

Strumming Chords with Non-Adjacent Strings

There are several instances when the notes of a chord will be spread across non-adjacent strings as well. Inversions are common in this regard, as are "add" or "sus" chords. Again, if you want to strum them, you can't get around fret-hand muting. Let's take a look at several common chords that present this problem. The same process applies to these chords. Mute the unwanted strings with the tips of fingers (or the thumb) on an adjacent string.

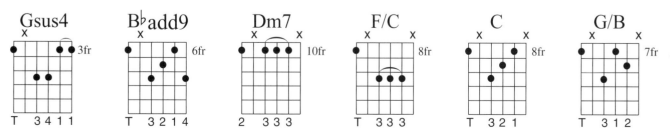

Let's hear those chords in action.

Example 3

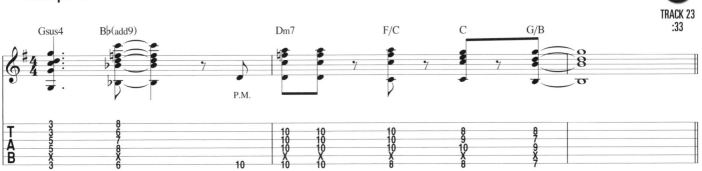

Muting is something that reveals itself necessary when the time comes. It allows freedom in the pick hand in many situations, and it will help keep your chords, licks, and riffs sounding lean, mean, and clean.

SUGGESTED LISTENING

Stevie Ray Vaughan: "Pride and Joy," "Couldn't Stand the Weather"

Jimi Hendrix: "Machine Gun," "Castles Made of Sand"

Extreme: "Decadence Dance," "Get the Funk Out"

Van Halen: "Black and Blue"

Smashing Pumpkins: "Cherub Rock"

HARMONICS

Harmonics have fascinated guitarists for generations, and it's no wonder. There's a brilliance to their tone, and the mechanics of them seem a bit magical. Though there are many forms of harmonics possible on the guitar, we won't be able to study them all. However, we will cover the ones that are essential to rock guitar, including: *natural harmonics*, *pinch harmonics*, and *tapped harmonics*. These three techniques have dressed up some of the most classic riffs and licks from players like Randy Rhoads, Eddie Van Halen, Zakk Wylde, Billy Gibbons, and countless more.

Technical Talk

Natural Harmonics

Natural harmonics are normally the first type learned on the guitar. They sound great both clean and distorted, they're relatively easy to master, and they're extremely versatile. To play a natural harmonic, you touch the string—but don't push it down to the fretboard—at specific points (called *nodes*), pluck the string, and then quickly remove your finger. You can touch at different places along the string to produce different pitches. The most important thing to remember is that you should touch the string *directly over the fretwire*—not slightly behind it as in normal fretting technique—for the clearest tone.

To play this twelfth-fret harmonic on the fourth string, for example, lightly touch the D string directly over the twelfth fret, pluck the string, and then immediately remove your finger. The result is a bell-like tone that's one octave above the open string.

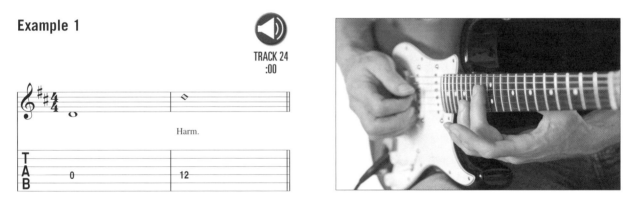

Example 1

TRACK 24
:00

Harm.

The twelfth-fret natural harmonic is the lowest pitched harmonic you can produce on a given string; any other natural harmonic produced on that string will be higher in pitch. This is because the twelfth fret is exactly the half point between the nut and the bridge. By touching the string at this node, you're dividing the length of the string in half, so to speak, causing it to sound an octave higher. By touching the string at other nodes, you're dividing the string into smaller fractions, which continue to raise the pitch of the harmonics. It's beyond the scope of this book to go into the science behind all of this, but the short story is that the available harmonic nodes on any string follow the *harmonic series*. A quick online search on the subject should shed some light on this.

Here's a table of the most commonly used natural harmonics available on each open string and the note they produce relative to the open string. The closer you get to the nut (or the bridge—these harmonics can be played as a mirror image proceeding toward the bridge), the higher the pitches get and the more difficult they are to sound. Distortion and/or compression will aid in this.

Fret of Harmonic	Pitch Produced
12	One octave higher
7	One octave and a 5th higher
5	Two octaves higher
4	Two octaves and a major 3rd higher

Pinch Harmonics

Pinch harmonics (also known as "pick harmonics" or "squeals") are actually one of several types of *artificial harmonics*. What's an artificial harmonic? Simple. An artificial harmonic is any harmonic that's not a natural harmonic. With artificial harmonics, we're fretting notes normally with our fret hand and using a special technique with our pick hand to sound the harmonic.

In terms of the pinch harmonic, we fret any note (though you can actually create a pinch harmonic on an open string as well) and allow the thumb of our pick hand to make contact with the string as we pick it. It will take a bit of practice to get a feel for it, but eventually you should be able to produce a squeal-like effect.

The use of distortion and humbucking pickups will greatly enhance the effect and make it much easier to sound the harmonics. Depending on where you're picking along the string, you can create different pitched harmonics without changing the fretted note at all. Listen to this example, where we're creating several different pitch harmonics all on this fretted A note on the fourth string.

Example 2

TRACK 24
:12

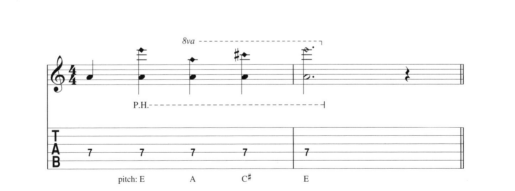

To hear absolute mastery of this technique in a hard rock or metal context, listen to Zakk Wylde. For a bluesy take on the technique, ZZ Top's Billy Gibbons is the one to check out. He even makes occasional use of a peso to produce his trademark squeals.

Tapped Harmonics

Another type of artificial harmonic is the tapped variety. There are a few different variations of this technique that we'll look at. The basic technique involves fretting a note and then quickly and forcefully tapping the string a specific distance of frets higher to sound a harmonic. The most common tapped harmonic is twelve frets higher, which creates a harmonic one octave higher than the fretted note. As with natural harmonics, the trick is to tap directly above the fretwire to sound the harmonic clearly. Also, don't push the string down to the fretboard. You want to quickly touch the string and then get off of it instantly, as if it were a hot stove burner. As with standard tapping technique (see Tapping chapter), there's not one standard with regards to which finger is used; some players tap harmonics with their first finger—either palming the pick or putting it in their mouth—while others use their second finger.

One variety of this technique, which is sometimes called a *touch harmonic*, involves picking a note normally and then touching or tapping the string at the specified fret to sound the harmonic. This is very common with a harmonic twelve frets above. It sounds like this.

Example 3

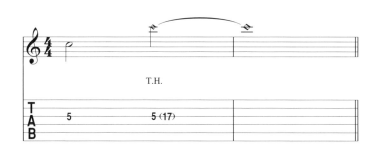

TRACK 24
:21

Another variety is to not use the pick at all. You sound the harmonic right off by silently fretting and tapping the specified fret immediately. That sounds like this.

Example 4

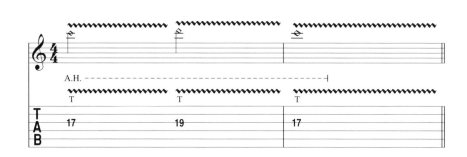

TRACK 24
:32

A third commonly used method is sometimes called the *slap harmonic*. Basically, this is just like the previous method except that you'll be slapping several strings to create a chord with harmonics. Obviously, barred shapes work best, because you can't bend your tapping finger, but you can get pretty close with other triad shapes as well, as demonstrated here.

Example 5

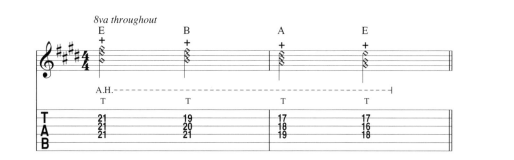

TRACK 24
:42

It'd be hard to argue that anyone has mastered the tapped harmonic technique more thoroughly than Eddie Van Halen. He makes them look as easy as breathing, and that's certainly often not the case—especially when you're tapping a harmonic only five frets up from the fretted note. To hear mastery of slap harmonics, also check out Eric Johnson.

Exercises

Let's work through these techniques with some exercises to get them under your fingers.

Natural Harmonics

Natural harmonics will sound great with a clean or distorted tone. This first exercise will give you a workout on the most commonly used natural harmonics: frets 12, 7, and 5.

Example 6

TRACK 25
:00

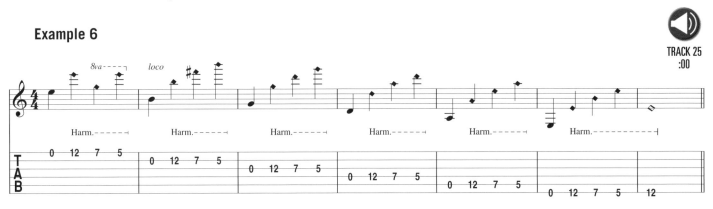

And now let's add the fourth fret harmonic into the fold. Picking closer to the bridge will help to bring it out.

Example 7

TRACK 25
:25

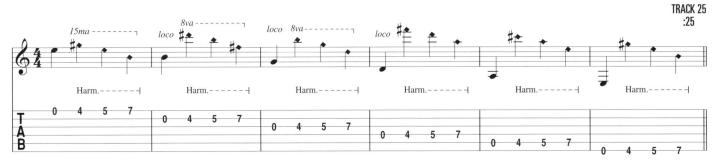

Pinch Harmonics

Pinch harmonics are most commonly played on strings 6–3, though you occasionally see them on the higher strings too. Here's an exercise to work on the basic technique.

Example 8

TRACK 26
:00

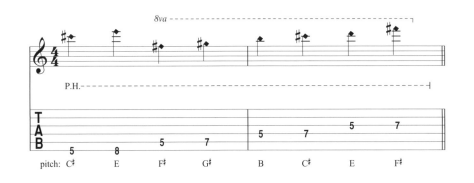

Now let's try to get more specific with the harmonic pitches we produce. You'll need to learn the location along the strings to produce the harmonic you want for a particular fretted note. Many times, a specific harmonic isn't always aimed for (they tend to sound pretty cool even when the harmonic isn't all that harmonious within the context of the song), but it's nice to be able to produce the same one repeatedly if you want.

Example 9

TRACK 26
:11

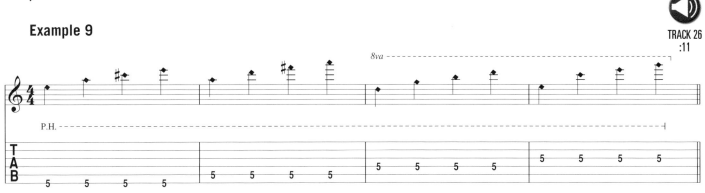

Tapped Harmonics

Here's an exercise in A minor that works on the touch harmonic. After hammering on with your left hand, touch the string lightly (and then get off it!) twelve frets higher directly over the fretwire.

Example 10

TRACK 27
:00

And here we're playing through an entire G minor pentatonic scale using tapped harmonics twelve frets up. You have to be very precise with your taps; otherwise, you'll get all kinds of unwanted noise.

Example 11

TRACK 27
:14

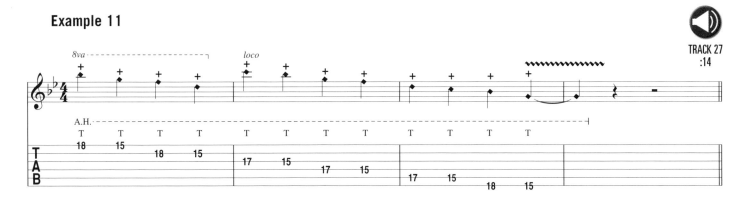

Now let's try tapping twelve, seven, and five frets up to get different pitched harmonics. These are a bit tougher.

Example 12

TRACK 27
:27

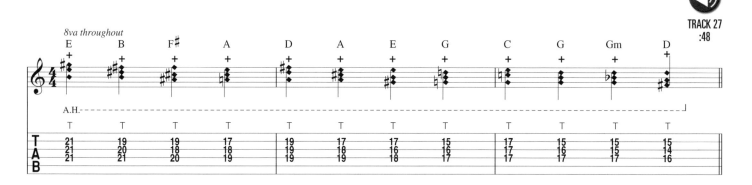

This exercise will work on the slap harmonic variety. Again, it's tough to get every note to come out perfectly clear, but do your best.

Example 13

TRACK 27
:48

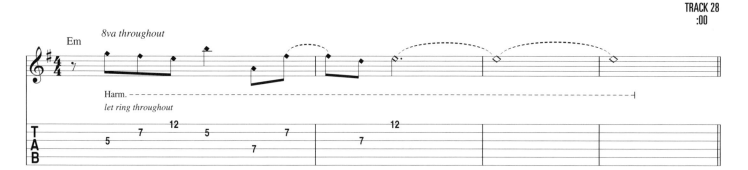

Licks

Now it's time for some licks using our newfound harmonic skills. We'll get to combine several different harmonic techniques in some of these. This first one is a nice melody in E minor created with all natural harmonics. It sounds great over an E pedal tone, as demonstrated on the audio via a second overdubbed guitar.

Example 14

TRACK 28
:00

The fourth, fifth, and seventh fret natural harmonics are great for coming up with interesting melodies. That's the method behind the madness of Example 15.

Example 15

TRACK 28
:16

Here's a bluesy rock lick that makes use of pinch harmonics galore. It's kind of a Billy Gibbons meets Zakk Wylde meets Joe Satriani thing. Feel free to try to recreate the harmonic pitches exactly, but it will probably sound just as cool with other ones too.

Example 16

TRACK 28
:50

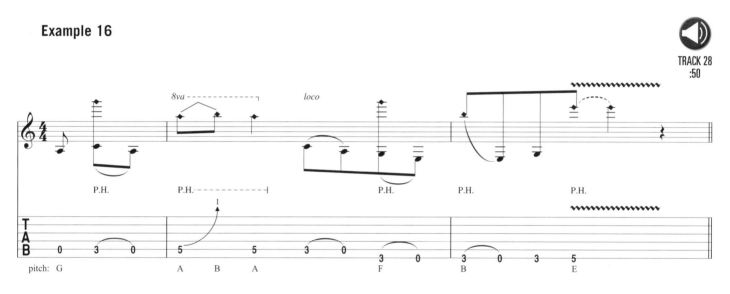

Here's a tapped harmonic buffet in C that makes use of harmonics five, seven, and nine frets above fretted notes.

Example 17

TRACK 28
:58

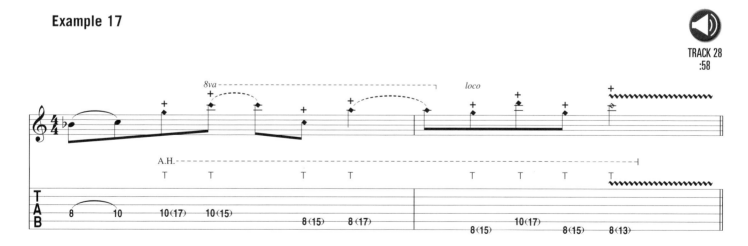

In this final lick, we're going to combine all three types of harmonics. Besides the fact that it sounds good, this lick will also help demonstrate some of the logistical concerns that arise when moving between several techniques in tandem like this. For instance, moving from measure 2 to measure 3, you only have one beat to move back into tapped harmonics after performing a pinch harmonic on the sixth string. If you tap harmonics with your first finger, you'll need to develop the coordination necessary to palm the pick and re-grip it quickly.

Example 18

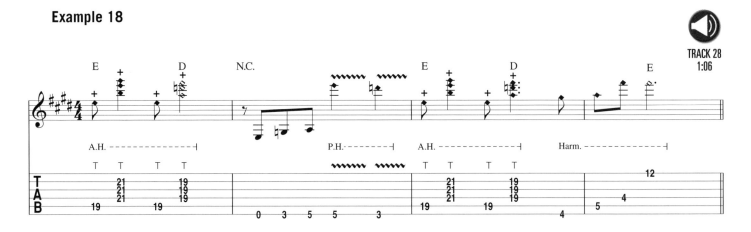

TRACK 28
1:06

SUGGESTED LISTENING

Van Halen: "Panama," "Hot for Teacher," "Summer Nights," "Dance the Night Away"

ZZ Top: "La Grange," "Sharp Dressed Man"

Ozzy Osbourne: "Crazy Babies"

Steve Vai: "The Animal," "Sisters"

Eric Johnson: "Trademark"

HYBRID PICKING

The term "hybrid picking" is often misunderstood, but the definition is actually fairly simple. It's the use of both a pick and fingers to pluck the strings. This can be accomplished with a standard flatpick and fingers or with a thumbpick and fingers. In today's rock world, the thumbpick isn't all that common, but it is still used quite a bit by country and rockabilly pickers; session virtuoso Brent Mason is an excellent example in the country world.

Hybrid picking is an extremely useful and versatile technique that opens up several new doors with regards to setting strings in motion. Players such as Eric Johnson, Zakk Wylde, Greg Harrison, and George Harrison make it a regular part of their arsenal, and you should too! With hybrid picking, you can:

* Simulate a piano-like attack with all notes sounding at the same time

* Easily move from fingerpicked arpeggio parts to standard picking instantaneously

* Pull off wide-interval string skipping lines at high speeds with little effort in the pick hand

* Add a southern, country flair to your playing

Technical Talk

With hybrid picking, you don't change the way you operate for normal picking at all. You're only going to add to that with the middle and ring fingers of your picking hand. (The pinky can be used occasionally as well, but it's not terribly common.) If you're already adept at fingerstyle technique, the transition to hybrid picking should be a fairly easy one. If you're totally new to fingerpicking altogether, don't worry; it's really not all that difficult.

You'll be using your middle and ring fingers to pluck (up toward your head) higher strings while using your pick on lower strings. This is an extreme generalization, however, and should not be thought of as any kind of rule. A good starting point for the hybrid technique is with your pick on string 4 and your middle and ring fingers on strings 3 and 2, respectively.

There really isn't one set rule with hybrid picking, and players generally adapt the technique to suit their needs. Having said that, there are several basic applications that are common enough to merit individual study.

Chordal Playing

One common use for the technique is to simply pluck the notes of a chord simultaneously instead of strumming them all with the pick. Obviously, you won't be able to do this with six-string chords, as you won't have enough digits to pluck all the strings. Therefore, this is most common with triads and other three-note chords.

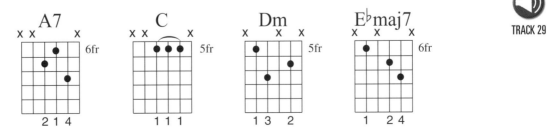

TRACK 29

Note that, with chords that contain non-adjacent strings (such as the open-voiced Dm triad), some players prefer to use pick/middle/ring while others prefer to incorporate their pinky in place of their ring finger due to the increased spacing.

Double Stops

Another very common use for hybrid picking is double stops. Many players will opt to pick them with middle and ring fingers because of the snappy sound it produces and/or because it can simulate an organ/piano-type attack. This is particularly common when double stops are volleyed against a lower note, which would be plucked with a downstroke of the pick, as demonstrated in the following phrase.

Example 1

TRACK 30
:00

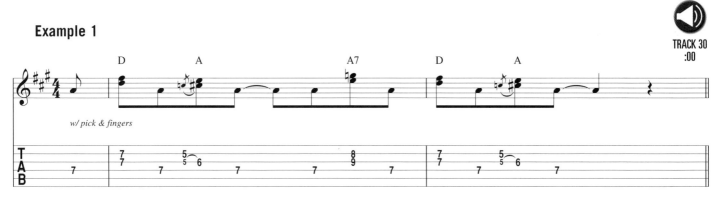

When playing 6ths, players often incorporate the hybrid picking technique as well for a crisp, clean sound.

Example 2

TRACK 30
:09

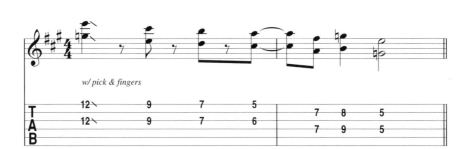

Arpeggiation

Hybrid picking also offers an option for intricate arpeggios that may be a bit too fast to play with a pick alone. This is especially useful if the part either precedes or follows another part that's played entirely with a pick. For example, if you want to follow this arpeggiated passage with a chunky power chord riff, hybrid picking will serve you well.

Example 3

TRACK 30
:19

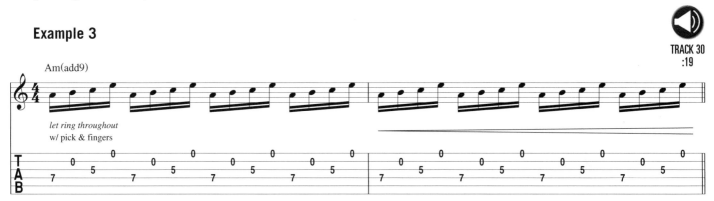

Country-Inspired Lines

The twang of country has infected many a rock player (including Zakk Wylde), and hybrid picking is the technique of choice for getting that sound. Many times, lines are arranged in a fashion similar to that of Example 1, with notes on a lower string taken with a downstroke of the pick and notes on a higher string plucked with the fingers. Example 4 is just such a phrase.

Example 4

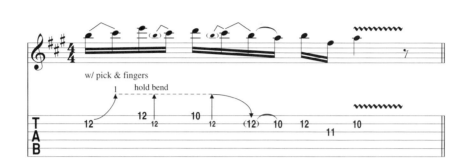

TRACK 30
:30

Exercises

Let's work on getting the technique down with some exercises. Example 5 works through several different inversions of a C chord with adjacent and non-adjacent string groups. Try to make all three notes of each chord speak equally well.

Example 5

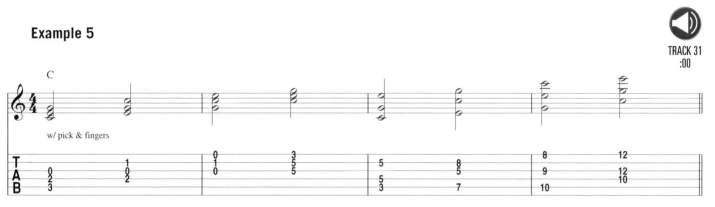

TRACK 31
:00

Here we're harmonizing an F major scale in triads, arranged in groups of two notes on top and one on bottom. We're also switching the order of the notes (bottom-top, top-bottom) for each triad.

Example 6

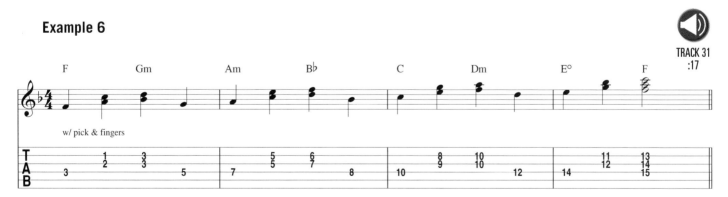

TRACK 31
:17

In this exercise, we work through the same harmonized F major scale, except we're arpeggiating each triad—pick, middle, ring on the way up and ring, middle, pick on the way down.

Example 7

TRACK 31
:33

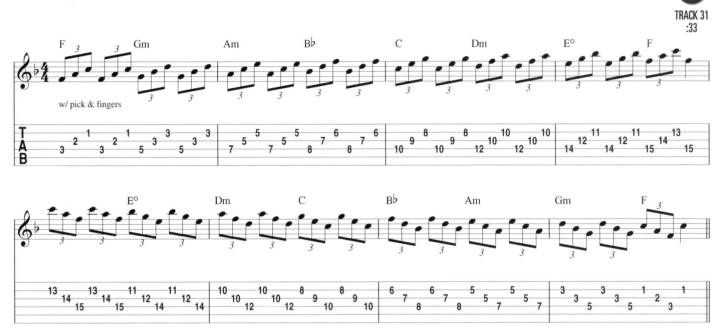

Here we're working up through the inversions of a G major chord and down through an Am chord with skipped strings throughout. All the intervals are either 6ths or 5ths.

Example 8

TRACK 32
:00

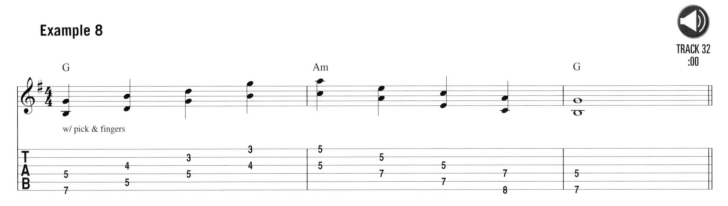

In Example 9, we're working double stops played with the fingers against a low root note played with the pick, but we're moving between string sets for the double stops. Though it would be possible to use the ring and pinky for strings 2 and 1, most players would simply move the middle and ring fingers back and forth between the two string sets.

Example 9

TRACK 32
:14

Here's an example that will help in beginning to incorporate hybrid picking into your lead lines. All the picked notes on the fifth fret should be plucked with your middle finger. All the notes on the seventh and eighth frets should be played with a downstroke of the pick. With practice, you can burn through these types of things effortlessly.

Example 10

TRACK 32
:28

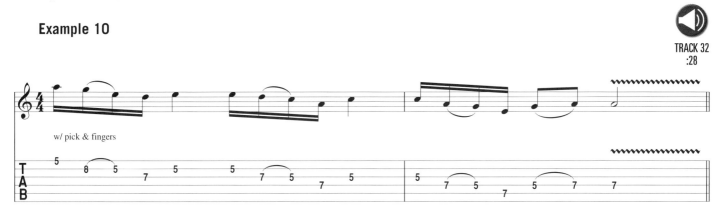

Here's another southern-flavored exercise that works on the double-stop/root notes separation. Pick all the notes on strings 3 and 2 with the middle and ring fingers, respectively, and all the notes on string 4 with the pick.

Example 11

TRACK 32
:44

Riffs & Licks

Let's put our hybrid picking to use now with some riffs and licks. Our first is a chordal riff in the vein of Eric Johnson. It's all played on the same string group, so it shouldn't be too challenging.

Example 12

TRACK 33
:00

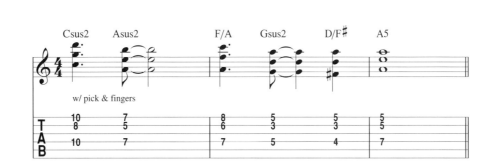

And here's a nice arpeggio idea in the key of C that keeps the middle and ring fingers planted on strings 3 and 2 while the pick wanders about among the lower strings.

Example 13

TRACK 33
:11

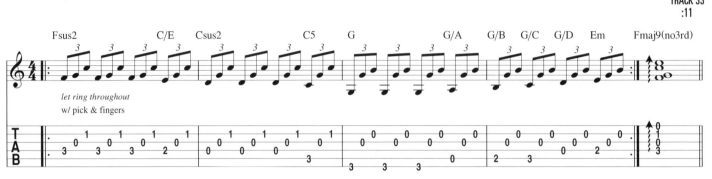

Example 14 is a southern-fried double-stop workout in C that will put your hybrid picking skills to the test. The trick with this kind of lick is to not get lost with regards to the rhythm. With hybrid picking, you're often not pairing downstrokes with downbeats, so you have to be a bit more aware of where you are in the measure.

Example 14

TRACK 33
:42

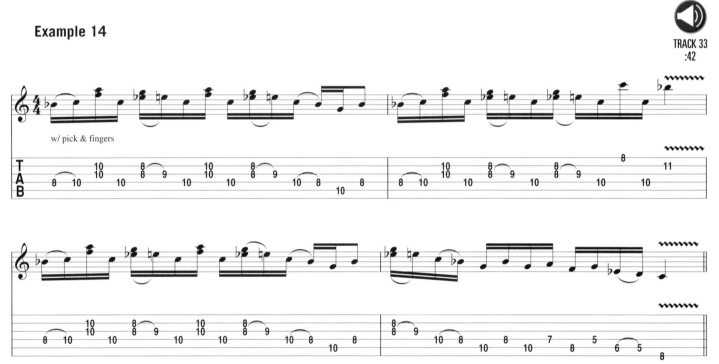

Here's a burning C minor lick that sequences mostly 4ths down the pentatonic scale. You're alternating with your middle finger and pick throughout.

Example 15

TRACK 34
:00

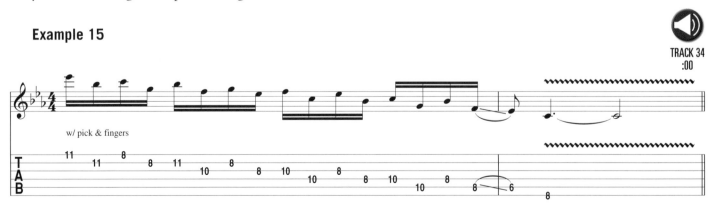

And here's a D minor scale pivot lick that's a nice showstopper. Aside from the final measure, the only notes played with the pick are the D notes at fret 12 on string 4.

Example 16

TRACK 34
:17

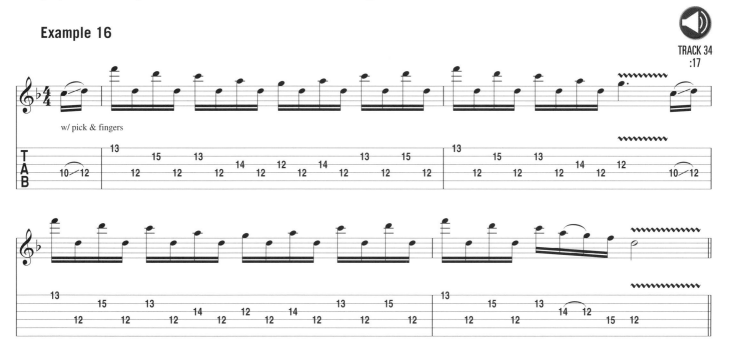

For our final lick, we'll check out a bit more of an advanced application of the technique. Here, we're keeping a steady quarter-note pulse on the open low E string with the pick while we peck out an E minor pentatonic melody on top. Notice that, with the addition of vibrato to the melody, we can really set the two voices apart and create the illusion of two guitars playing at once.

Example 17

TRACK 34
:45

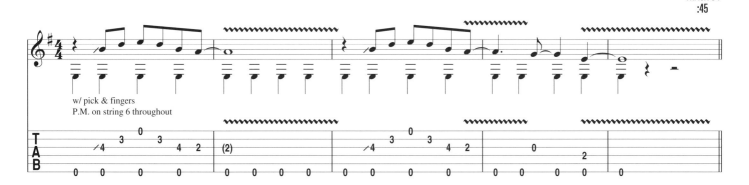

SUGGESTED LISTENING

Eric Johnson: "Zap," "Cliffs of Dover," "Trademark"

Ratt: "Way Cool Jr."

Creedence Clearwater Revival: "Green River"

The Beatles: "Help," "All My Loving"

LEGATO

The legato technique is a large one to tackle, since its definition is so broad. It basically means that two (or more) notes are connected where only the first one is picked (or plucked). On the guitar, we accomplish this with a variety of means—namely hammer-ons, pull-offs, and slides. (Tapping is technically a legato technique as well, but we'll cover that in depth in its own chapter.)

Long strings of legato notes weren't very common in the early days of rock 'n' roll. The limited sustain of the cleaner amp tones back then didn't make them speak very well. But as time progressed, more and more distortion became available to the rock guitarist. This led naturally to more sustain, which in turn led to more exploitation of the legato technique. By the seventies, players were regularly churning out lines drenched in hammer-ons, pull-offs, and slides. By the time the guitar solo hit its heyday in the eighties, there were players that had mastered the technique beyond belief, including Eddie Van Halen, Joe Satriani, and Steve Vai. And if you've never checked out fusion virtuoso Allan Holdsworth in this regard, you're in for a jaw-dropping treat! The solo to "Devil Take the Hindmost" from his *Metal Fatigue* album is simply one of the most wicked examples of legato guitar playing ever.

Technical Talk

As mentioned earlier, we'll look at three main techniques under the legato umbrella: hammer-ons, pull-offs, and slides. Each one is integral in creating those long, serpentine lines favored by players such as those listed above.

Hammer-ons

Hammer-ons are usually the easiest for the beginner, and the concept is fairly simple. You pick a note and then "hammer" down onto a higher note on the same string with another finger. You'll need to make the motion swift and forceful and remember to maintain pressure on the string with the hammered finger. The use of gain will make the hammered note speak easier, but you should eventually be able to accomplish this with the cleanest of guitar tones. In this example, we pick the G note on fret 5 of string 4, which is fretted with the index finger, and then hammer down with the ring finger onto the A note at fret 7.

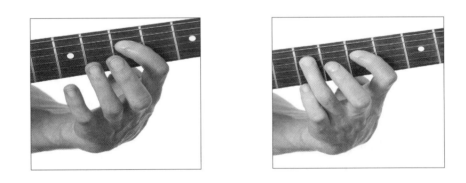

Example 1

TRACK 35
:00

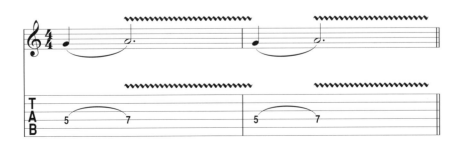

Pull-offs

The pull-off is kind of the opposite of the hammer-on, but really only in the fact that one ascends in pitch and the other descends. The techniques used to accomplish each are quite different from each other. With a pull-off, you'll need to fret both notes at once—a higher note and a lower note on the same string. You pick the higher note and then "pull off" the string so that the lower note sounds. You're essentially plucking the string with the pull-off finger. You'll need to pull slightly down—as opposed to straight up—in order for the low pitch to sound clearly. With practice, you'll develop a motion that's efficient in movement and sound production.

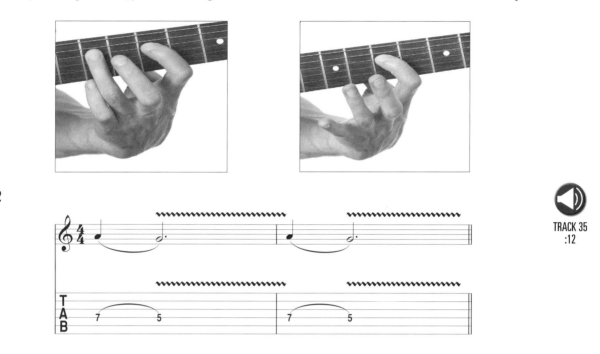

Example 2

TRACK 35
:12

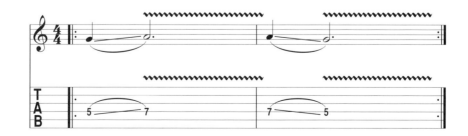

Slides

Slides are just about as pure of a legato sound as we can create on the guitar, with the exception of actually wearing a slide on our finger (see Slide chapter). With the slide technique, we're literally sliding one finger up and down the string to sound the notes. This means that we hear all the notes in between the starting and target notes. Slides can be one fret in distance, continue for as many frets as you have on your guitar, or anywhere in between. They can also be ascending and descending and be performed with any of the fret-hand fingers.

Be aware that there are two types of slides. They're often referred to as *picked slides* and *glisses* (or legato slides). Gliss is short for the Italian term "glissando," which means "to glide" (the Italian term is actually derived from the French "glisser"). In a picked slide, both the starting and target notes are picked. Therefore, it's not a legato technique. In a gliss, or legato slide, only the starting note is picked. We then slide our finger (maintaining pressure on the fretboard all along) to the target pitch without re-attacking it. Let's look at an example of both ascending and descending slides.

Example 3

TRACK 35
:23

With only two frets to cover, the slide isn't as obvious as it could be. When the slide covers a greater distance, the effect is a bit more dramatic.

Example 4

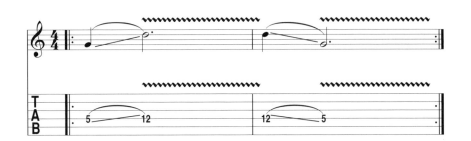

TRACK 35
:39

Exercises

These exercises are a considerable workout for your fretting hand, so be sure to stop and take breaks when necessary. It's also a good idea to stretch out your hands and forearms before tackling something like this. Be sure to use a metronome so that you develop a solid rhythm along with your legato technique. It's very easy to get into the habit of rushing (or dragging) certain finger combinations of hammer-ons and pull-offs.

Examples 5–7 will work out every hammer-on combination between your four fingers, while Examples 8–10 will do the same with pull-offs. Be sure to play them using every finger combination listed. Continue these up to the twelfth fret and then back down if you like. You'll likely find the ones that isolate your pinky and ring fingers to be particularly difficult, and the isolation of the pinky and middle finger won't be too much better. The pinky is definitely the weakest digit, and nothing demonstrates that more than legato playing.

Example 5

TRACK 36
:00

Example 6

TRACK 36
:14

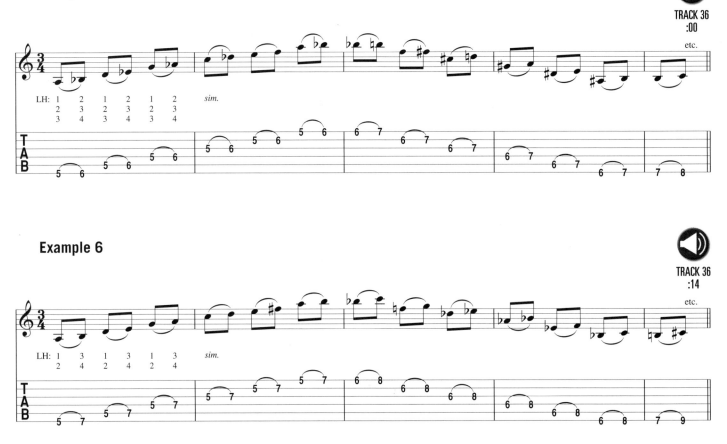

Example 7

TRACK 36
:27

Example 8

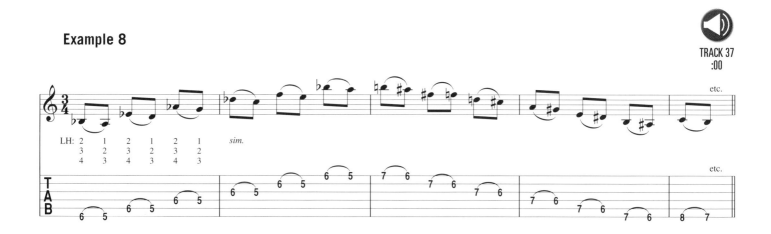

TRACK 37
:00

Example 9

TRACK 37
:14

Example 10

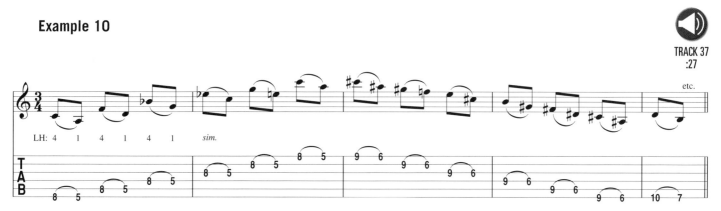

TRACK 37
:27

Examples 11 and 12 are particularly wicked exercises that combine hammer-ons and pull-offs together; although, 11 concentrates mostly on hammer-ons, while 12 concentrates mostly on pull-offs. The use of a metronome on these exercises is absolutely critical.

Example 11

TRACK 38
:00

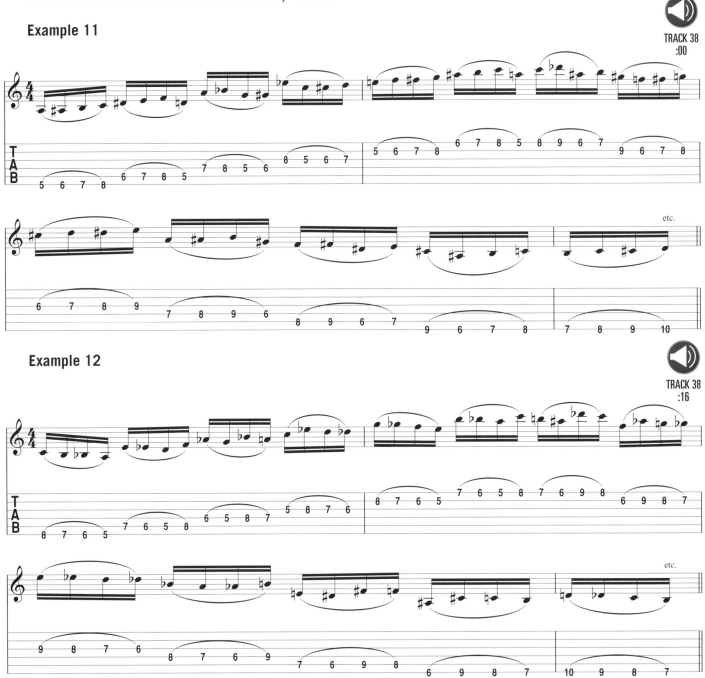

Example 12

TRACK 38
:16

Examples 13–14 work out the slide technique with consecutive half steps, whole steps, and a minor 3rd/ whole step combination. Again, execute the exercises with each finger, and try to visualize the slides as one complete, flowing motion.

Example 13

TRACK 39
:00

Example 14

TRACK 39
:18

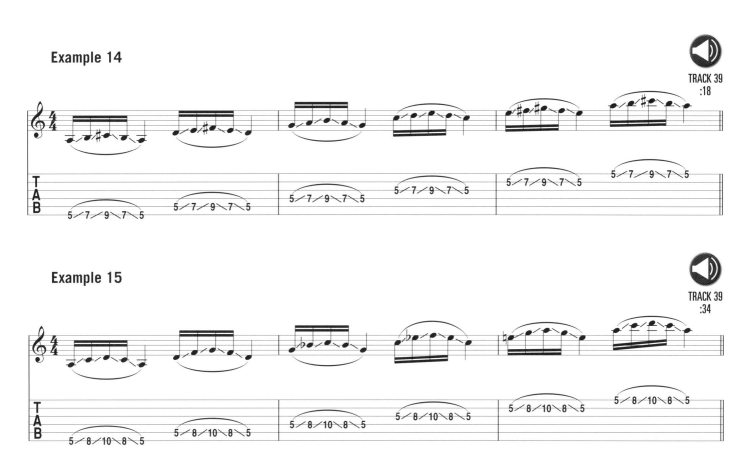

Example 15

TRACK 39
:34

These final two exercises combine hammer-ons, pull-offs, and slides all in one. Be sure to use the metronome and try your best to make each note clearly audible.

Example 16

TRACK 40
:00

Example 17

TRACK 40
:28

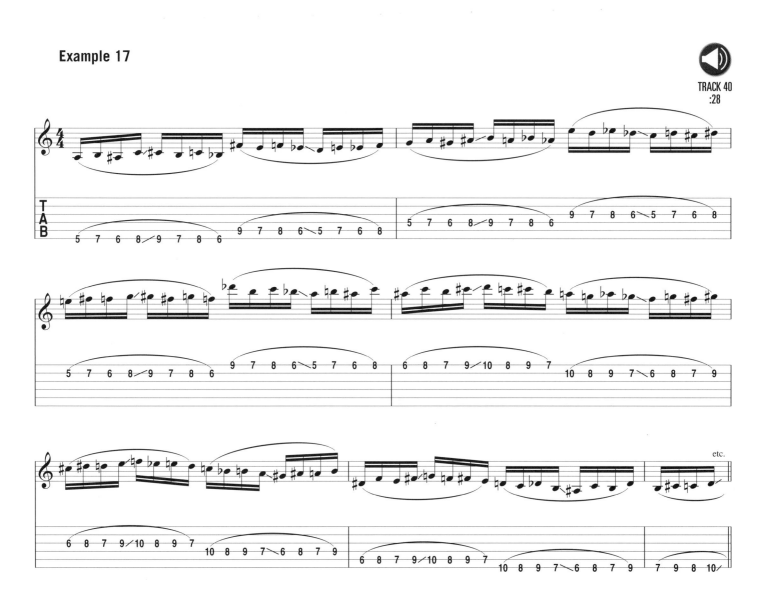

Licks

It's time to test your new legato skills with some slippery licks. Again, these will sound best with a good amount of gain. Our first is a rapid-fire sequence in E minor that works out pull-offs exclusively on the top two strings.

Example 18

TRACK 41
:00

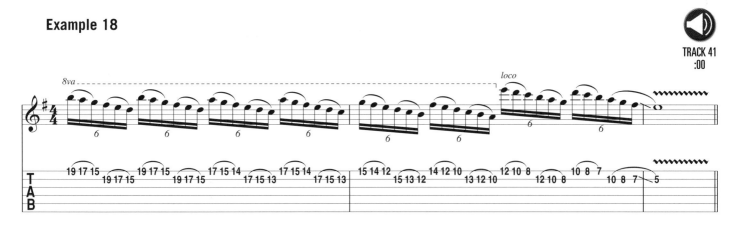

And here's a C Mixolydian lick that involves a bit of string skipping for a Paul Gilbert effect. On the final descent, be sure to keep the rhythm steady.

Example 19

TRACK 41
:25

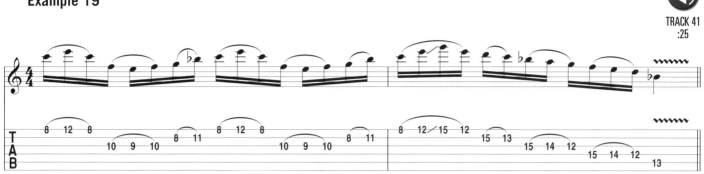

This is a D minor pentatonic lick that uses a legato technique called the "hammer-on from nowhere." You're only picking the first note of each descending phrase; after that, you simply hammer on to each lower string without picking it.

Example 20

TRACK 41
:42

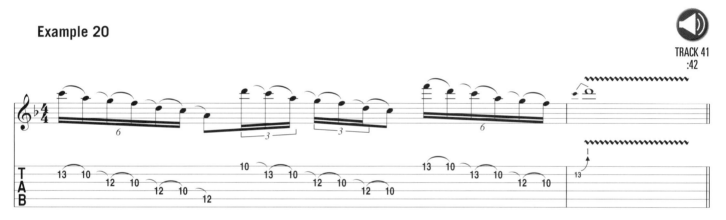

Example 21 is a slipping and sliding lick from the B minor pentatonic scale that moves the same sliding/hammering/pulling maneuver down through the scale in different string sets. Work this up to speed slowly until you've got the slides down; you're not always sliding the same distance!

Example 21

TRACK 42
:00

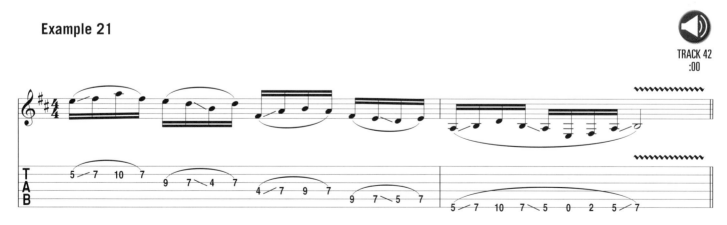

Here's a speedy lick in A harmonic minor that's reminiscent of the scary Swede Yngwie Malmsteen. You've got one position shift from E to F on string 1, but other than that this one's all hammer-ons and pull-offs.

Example 22

TRACK 42
:18

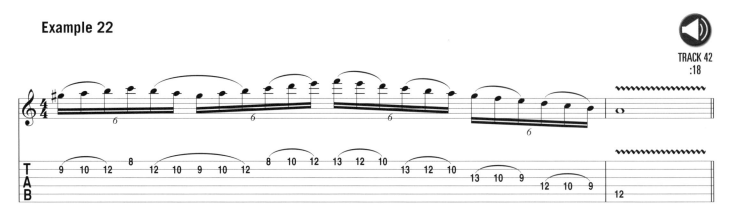

And finally, here's a jumbled ascending lick in D minor that uses three-note fragments in a hammer/pull fashion. You have to be careful not to make this lick sound like triplets; with the three-note groupings, that's easy to do.

Example 23

TRACK 42
:37

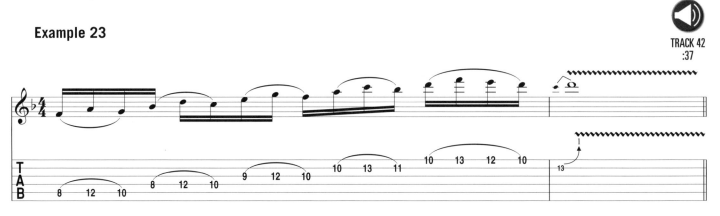

SUGGESTED LISTENING

Van Halen: "Ice Cream Man," "Drop Dead Legs"

Joe Satriani: "Always with Me, Always with You," "Mystical Potato Head Groove Thing"

Steve Vai: "Tender Surrender," "The Audience Is Listening"

Allan Holdsworth: "Devil Take the Hindmost"

ONE-FINGER POWER CHORDS (DROP D TUNING)

Ever since the Seattle crowd discovered Neil Young's precursor to the grunge sound with his seventies classics like "Cinnamon Girl," the one-fingered power chord has been a mainstay in modern rock. This chord, facilitated by drop D tuning (D–A–D–G–B–E, low to high) has been the perfect vehicle for not only the sludgy half-time riffs of Soundgarden, but also the frenzied, chaotic precision of bands like System of a Down.

If you've never messed around in drop D tuning before, be warned: the hours can quickly get away from you. After pounding out a full, open D chord for half an hour just because it sounds so good, you're likely to get seduced by the extra girth in your tone resulting from the slackened sixth string.

Technical Talk

First thing's first. Tune your sixth string down a whole step to D—you can just match the pitch of your fourth string (an octave lower, of course) for a quick fix if you don't have a tuner on hand. Now barre the low three strings at the third fret. Bingo! You're playing an F5 chord.

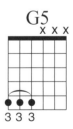

F5

You'll need to get acclimated to thinking "down a whole step" with regards to your low E string. If you've played in standard tuning your whole life, it will take a while to see the third fret of the sixth string as F instead of G. However, the fact that most songs in drop D tuning are also in the key of D will help with this immensely, as you'll be able to see the tonic scale along that string.

Flattened Fingers

Are you ready to really make your old classical teacher cringe? Since you can only slide around one finger so fast, many players, when performing lightning fast power chord riffs in drop D, use all four fingers to play chords at one time or another. For example, if you're moving quickly from the F5 chord at fret 3 to a G5 at fret 5, you may use your ring finger to fret the G5, which would look like this:

Connecting the two chords in the middle with an F♯5 chord might warrant the use of the second finger, and so on. It's basically as if you're playing notes on the low E string with the most horrid technique a classical guitar teacher can imagine! However, as I explained in the Fret-Hand Muting chapter, this is rock guitar—not classical guitar—and it's a perfectly valid technique for this purpose.

G5

Keep in mind that most players don't use this approach unless it's necessary. For slower riffs, most players will handle most of the chords with just one or maybe two fingers.

Riffs

Ok, let's get to the riffs. As mentioned, most of these will be in the key of D. Examples 1 and 2 demonstrate one of the coolest things about this concept; you can bank power chords up the neck off an open D5 power chord. Simulating this with a standard-tuned E5 chord in the key of E would be extremely difficult, if not impossible at faster tempos.

Example 1

TRACK 43
:00

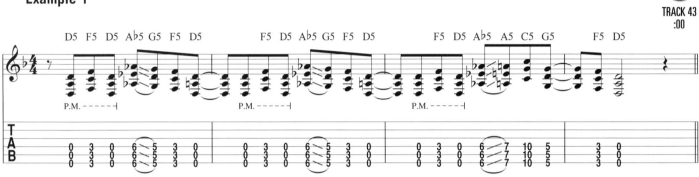

Example 2

TRACK 43
:13

In this next riff, we see another added benefit of the one-finger power chord: they're easily turned into a cool-sounding sus2 chord by adding one finger two frets higher on the fourth string.

Example 3

TRACK 44
:00

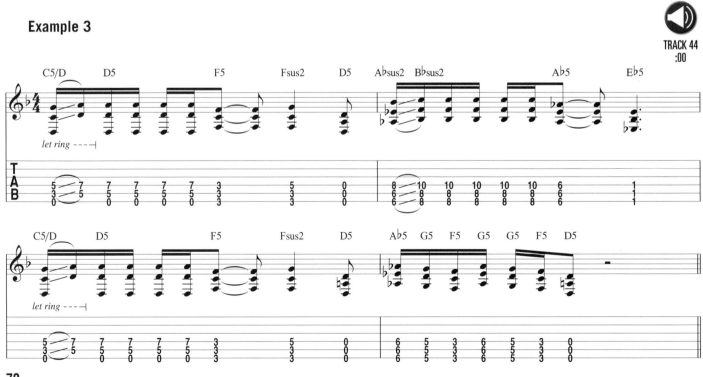

And not all drop D riffs have to be in the key of D, as is demonstrated by this Nirvana-styled riff in the key of A.

Example 4

SUGGESTED LISTENING

Neil Young: "Cinnamon Girl"

Soundgarden: "Outshined"

Steve Vai: "Bad Horsie"

Ozzy Osbourne: "No More Tears"

Nirvana: "Heart Shaped Box"

PICK-HAND MUTING

While much of the job of pick-hand muting goes unnoticed like fret-hand muting, at least the pick hand is responsible for one of the most ubiquitous sounds in all of rock guitar: the palm mute. However, the pick hand's role in muting is much more complex than simply chugging on a muted open low E string, as we'll soon find out.

The pick hand works in conjunction with the fret hand to keep unwanted noises from popping out amidst the hi-gain assault emitting from your instrument. Even a noise gate can only do so much—i.e., it can only keep things quiet when you stop playing. The rest of the responsibility of cleanliness lies in your hands—literally.

Technical Talk

Keeping the Rumble to a Minimum

With higher gain settings, noise will pipe up at every opportunity given. Therefore, the primary job of the pick hand in terms of muting is to keep the rumble of the lower strings under control when you're not playing them. This simply means that, if you're playing a note on the G string for instance, then you'd lay your palm on strings 6–4 to keep them from making noise. If you're playing on the B string, your palm would also cover string 3, and so on.

Playing on the G string while muting
lower strings with palm

Keep a Lid on It

Sustaining G string while holding
B and E strings with pick hand

Another aspect of pick-hand muting comes into play when you're sustaining notes on anything but the high E string. If you climax your solo with a high-energy bend on string 2 with vibrato, there's a good chance that the high E string will make some noise if it's not kept under control. This can easily be accomplished by touching the string with a pick-hand finger. If you're sustaining a note on the G string, you can hold both the E and B strings with the pick hand to keep them quiet. This will assure that, no matter how wicked the vibrato, the treble strings won't be nudged into noise.

The "Offs" Between the "Ons"

Another responsibility of the pick hand when playing with high gain is to be the "offs" between the "ons." Depending on your settings, it may only take a second or two for noise to creep in once you've stopped playing, so it's up to you to make sure that doesn't happen. Some people rely on a noise gate to take care of this, but they can sound unnatural at times. Besides, it's nice to not have to rely on a piece of equipment for such a fundamental aspect of clean playing; after all, what happens if you sit in somewhere and find yourself without your noise gate?

Laying palm on strings to keep them
quiet when not playing

The solution is simple. When you stop playing, simply lay your palm down on the strings. You can also (and should) reinforce this by laying your fret hand lightly on the strings to make sure absolutely no noise has a chance to creep in.

The Almighty Palm Mute

The final aspect of pick-hand muting, and the one that most people actually think of when they hear "muting" with regards to the pick hand, is the technique of *palm muting*. Simply put, heavy metal would not be possible without it! With palm muting, you allow the palm of the pick hand to touch the string just in front of the bridge while you're playing. The result is a muted, chunky sound. Though it's by far most common on the lower strings, it is used on the treble strings as well.

Palm muting on the
low E string

The farther in from the bridge you move your palm, the more muted and chunky the sound becomes. You can experiment with this to find the desired amount of mute for a specific riff or lick.

Exercises

Playing Cleanly

This first exercise is simply the E minor pentatonic scale in open position. The focus here is on having the palm follow the pick hand across the strings, keeping everything below the sounding string quiet.

Example 1

TRACK 45
:00

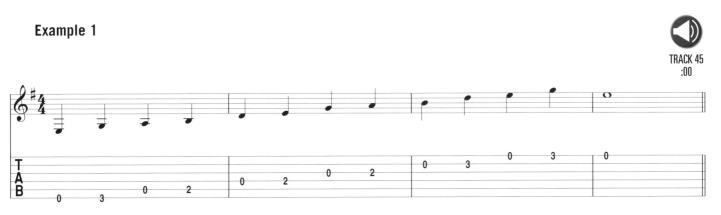

And here we're still ascending, but the notes on each string are reversed. You'll find that, unless you have very small hands, your fretting finger can most likely aid in the muting process by lightly touching the string below the one it's fretting. This will stop the open string from ringing out just as the new note is fretted. This, in combination with the pick hand doing its job, will ensure a clean phrase. You have to be careful though, especially if you have very large hands, that you don't accidentally fret the string below and cause it to sound.

Example 2

TRACK 45
:16

In Example 3, we're following low open strings with string skipping phrases. This one will test your pick-muting skills for sure.

Example 3

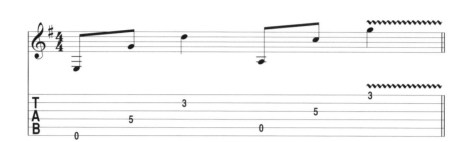

TRACK 45
:30

In this final exercise, we're pulling off notes to an open string, skipping up two strings, and repeating the process. Be sure that you can't hear the lower open string at all once you skip up two strings for the next note.

Example 4

TRACK 45
:38

Palm Muting

Examples 5 and 6 concentrate on alternating between standard picking and palm muting on the low strings. You'll do this type of thing quite a bit in the real musical world, so you have to get used to it.

Example 5

TRACK 46
:00

Example 6

TRACK 46
:14

And here we'll get some practice palm muting on the higher strings—not quite as common, but it still shows up, and it's a cool sound.

Example 7

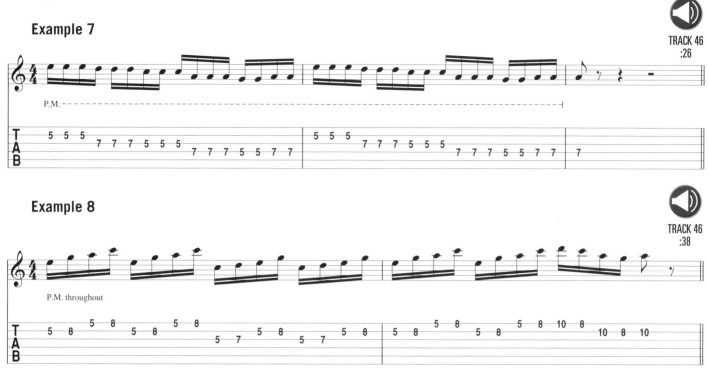

Example 8

Riffs & Licks

Ok now let's test out the pick hand with some riffs & licks that concentrate on muting. Our first lick is a wide-interval lick that covers a good bit of ground. Your pick hand will need to follow closely on the lower strings to keep them quiet.

Example 9

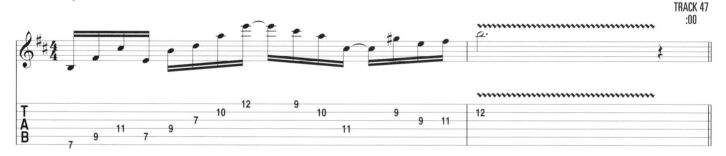

This one works with a lot of pull-offs to open strings, which are a common source of unwanted noise for many players. Be sure to mute the top strings with the pick hand while you're sustaining the final bend.

Example 10

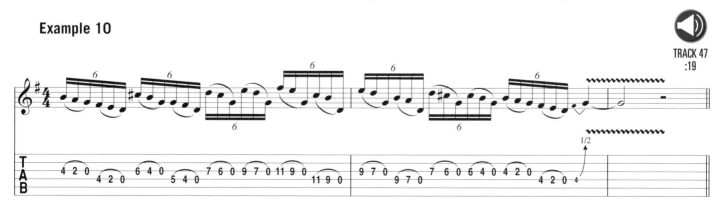

And here's a D minor string-skipping line in the style of Eric Johnson. Take it slowly at first until the muting becomes second nature.

Example 11

TRACK 47
:43

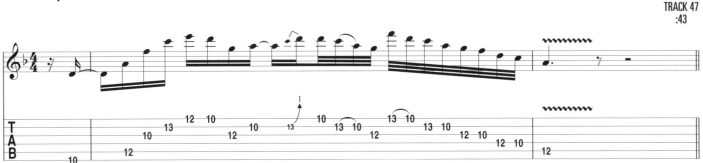

Now let's try this palm-muting riff, which sounds like something straight out of an eighties metal song. The palm-muted low E string with unmuted power chords above is a standard metal rhythm move.

Example 12

TRACK 48
:00

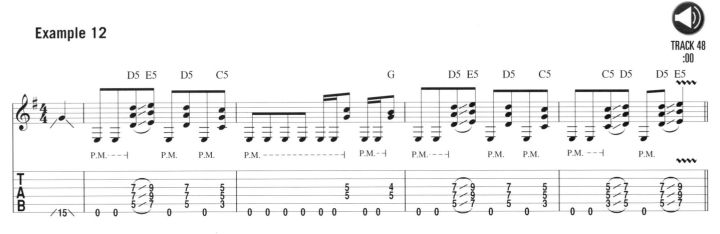

In Example 13, we see a similar strategy, except we're muting with the A string instead of the E. This is another common rhythmic device in hard rock and metal. We're using sixteenth notes here, so you'll really need to be able to shift back and forth between muted and not effortlessly.

Example 13

TRACK 48
:14

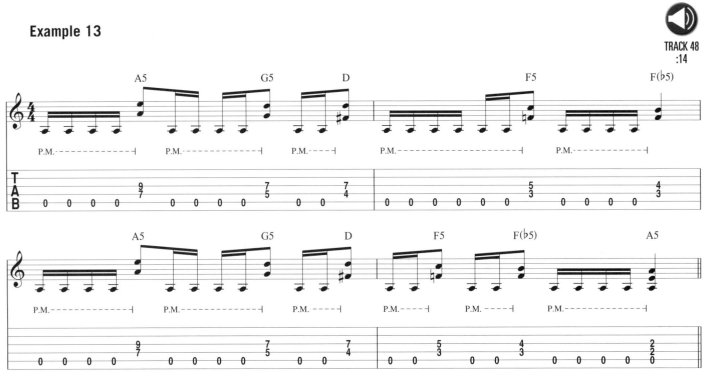

In this lick, we're mixing up palm-muted lines with normal notes for an ascending sequence in B minor. This type of thing can really breathe life into an otherwise typical line.

Example 14

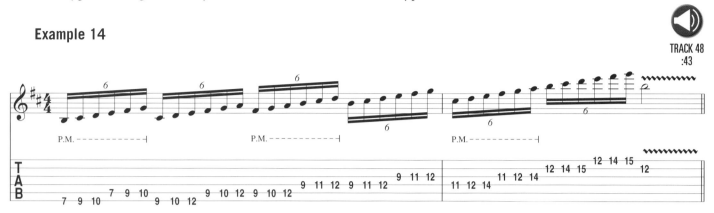

For our final lick, we're palm muting exclusively on the higher strings for a bluesy rock lick in A. The only note that's not muted is the final one.

Example 15

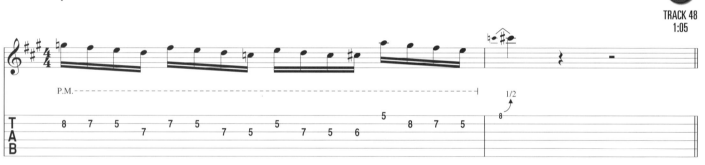

SUGGESTED LISTENING

Eric Johnson: "Cliffs of Dover," "Desert Rose," "Nothing Can Keep Me from You"

Steve Vai: "Tender Surrender," "Die to Live"

Metallica: "Master of Puppets," "One"

Ozzy Osbourne: "Crazy Train," "I Don't Know"

PICK SCRAPES

Whereas there was certainly a movement in the late eighties geared toward recognizing rock music (rock guitar) as serious endeavors worthy of classroom study, let's face it: sometimes rock guitar is just all about attitude and flash. With that sentiment, let's examine the *pick scrape* (also called the *pick slide*)—one of many unique noises and theatrical movements perpetuated by generations of rock guitarists.

Technical Talk

One might think the technique is pretty self-explanatory. I mean … you're *scraping* your *pick* along the strings to make a cool sound. How tough can it be, right? But there are several pointers that will help achieve maximum "scrapage."

- **Bass strings work best:** For the classic rock pick scrape, you'll want to scrape along the lowest strings—the sixth and fifth will produce awesome results every time.

- **Press into the strings while scraping:** This will provide some tension that will cause the pick to slightly catch on the grooves in the wound strings, which will help to enhance the effect.

- **Don't go too fast:** You don't need to traverse the entire length of the string. In fact, the sound produced will be most effective while you're over the pickups. You can finish off quickly with a flashy move down the length of the string, but if you want a nice, thick scrape to be audible, you'll want to spend most of the time in front of the neck.

Example 1 demonstrates the classic pick scrape. In the audio example, the entire length of the string is traveled for demonstration purposes. Notice how the effect is strongest in the beginning, when the pick is out in front of the neck.

Example 1

TRACK 49
:00

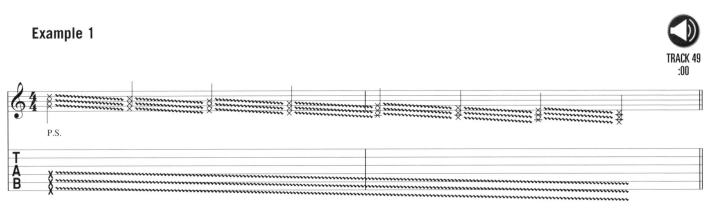

Riffs

Let's get our scrape on with some classic riffs. Our first is a typical use for the pick scrape: a dynamic intro with big, sustained power chords.

Example 2

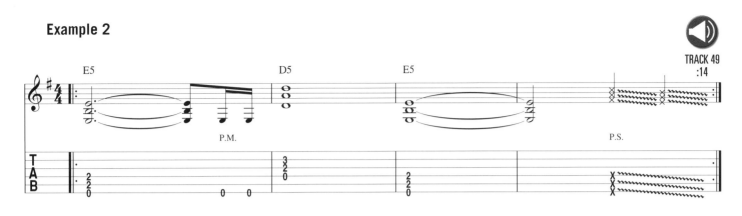

In this example, we're scraping back and forth in rhythm to create another type of scrape effect.

Example 3

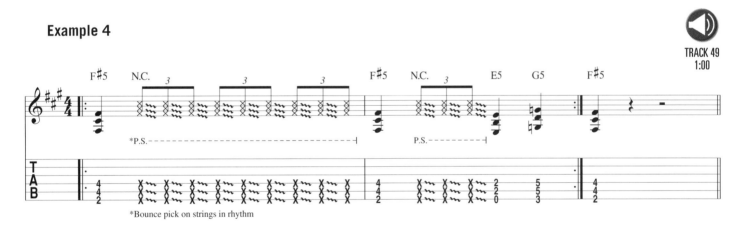

And Example 4 presents another option: the *bouncing scrape.* To produce this effect, quickly jab the strings with your pick in scrape position for a stuttering effect.

Example 4

*Bounce pick on strings in rhythm

There really are no rules when it comes to this kind of thing. You're just trying to make some cool noises. So unleash your child-like curiosity and experiment!

SUGGESTED LISTENING

Ozzy Osbourne: "Crazy Train"

Van Halen: "Panama," "You Really Got Me"

Steve Vai: "Greasy Kid Stuff"

Boston: "Don't Look Back"

RAKES

The *rake* is an expressive device employed by rock and blues guitarists for extra intensity and added sonic weight. Sometimes unintentional and other times completely deliberate, it's a technique that many players use without even knowing it. It's one of those subtle sounds that is hard to always detect but would certainly be missed if it weren't there. One listen to any solo by Stevie Ray Vaughan, Steve Vai, Joe Satriani, or Zakk Wylde, and you're bound to hear some well-placed rakes.

Technical Talk

Rakes are similar to grace notes in that they don't take up any real time. They're almost always used as a last-second pickup into a note that needs some extra zing. Though the ascending rake is much more common, they can be descending as well. Interestingly, the technique used for each is quite different.

Ascending Rakes

In an ascending rake, we're essentially strumming up through several deadened (or muted) strings on the way to our target note, which is often on the first, second, or third string. The strings below this target note are muted by the palm (see the Pick-Hand Muting chapter), a fret-hand finger (see the Fret-Hand Muting chapter), or a combination of both to keep them quiet, and the pick is dragged across them deliberately to produce a percussive, clicking sound. This is usually done fairly quickly, so the individual clicks of the muted strings blur together into one "bpttttt" sound.

Pick hand in preparation to rake up into a note on the B string

Example 1 demonstrates the sound of a normal note followed by the same note with an ascending rake.

Example 1

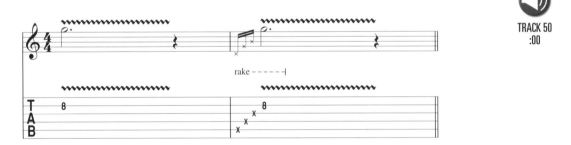

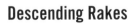

TRACK 50
:00

Descending Rakes

Whereas the ascending rakes are normally performed with notes on the top three strings, it stands to reason that descending rakes are normally performed with notes on the bottom three strings. In a descending rake, you'll be strumming up through muted strings on your way to a target note on a lower string. However, this time the strings are muted with your fretting hand—usually by the underside of the first, second, or third finger (see the Fret-Hand Muting chapter). Because of this, the sound produced is slightly different than the ascending rake, but the effect is similar.

Pick hand in preparation to rake down into a note on the D string

Here's an example of a normal note on the D string followed by the same with a descending rake.

Example 2

TRACK 50
:09

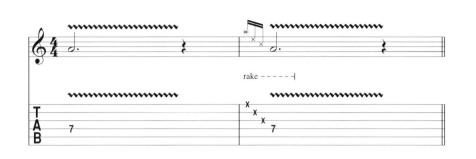

Note: The terms "up" and "down" may be slightly confusing if you're thinking solely of physical direction. In this instance, the terms refer to the orientation of the guitar's pitches, where the thinner strings are called the high strings, and the thicker strings are called the low strings. So, an ascending rake, while going from low to high *in pitch*, actually involves moving the pick *down* toward the floor—vice versa for a descending rake.

Exercises

Let's work through a few exercises to get a feel for this. Example 3 works down an A minor pentatonic scale from C on string 1 to A on string 4. We use ascending rakes on every single note. Be sure the only clear pitches you're hearing are the target notes.

Example 3

TRACK 51
:00

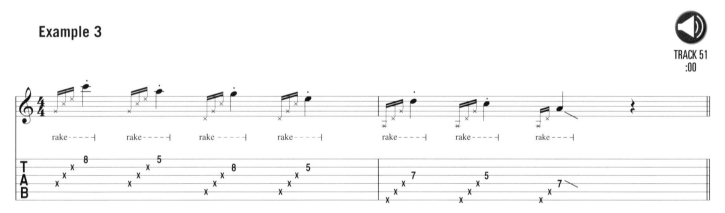

And now let's travel up an A minor pentatonic scale to string 3, using descending rakes on every note.

Example 4

TRACK 51
:11

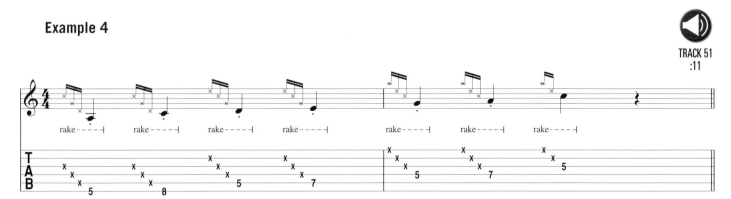

In this last exercise, we're alternating ascending and descending rakes. Listen carefully for extraneous, unwanted noises!

Example 5

TRACK 51
:20

Licks

Ok, let's put these rakes to use in some licks. One of the most dramatic uses for the descending rake is the open E string. Jimi Hendrix and Stevie Ray would make use of this often. Check it out.

Example 6

TRACK 52
:00

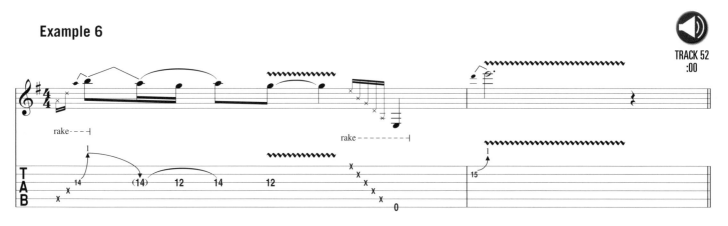

Here's a classic use for the ascending rake: a note on the B string bent up a whole step to the tonic of a minor pentatonic scale. This one's been used by just about everyone who's ever played a blues scale.

Example 7

TRACK 52
:11

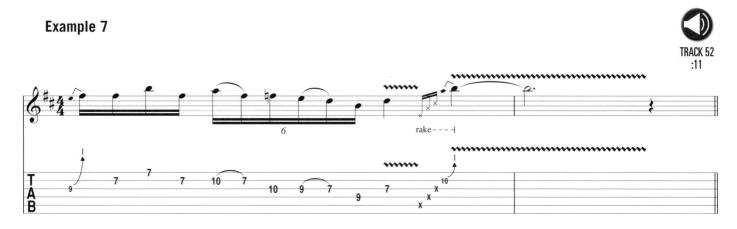

Here's a page from the B.B. King playbook. This trick has been called the "octave yelp." Use your pinky for the high A note. Why? Well, in addition to the pick hand muting strings 6–2, the first finger of the fret hand can quiet the strings as well (or instead).

Example 8

TRACK 52
:20

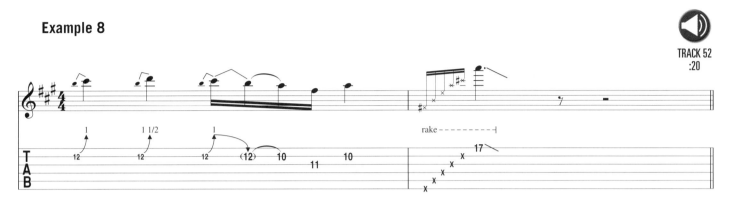

For our final lick, here's something Zakk Wylde might do. This is a series of repeated, screaming bends on the second and third strings with massive rakes and exaggerated vibrato. Pull this one out, and your guitar will sound as though it's about to explode.

Example 9

TRACK 52
:30

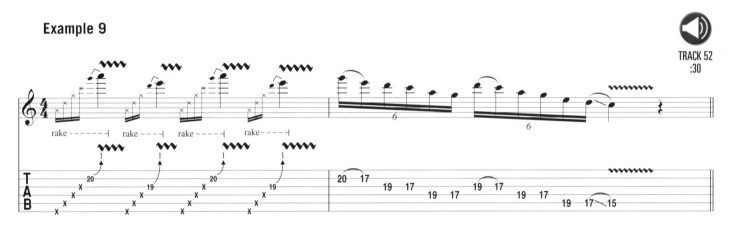

SUGGESTED LISTENING

Ozzy Osbourne: "Miracle Man"

Van Halen: "Eruption"

Steve Vai: "For the Love of God"

Stevie Ray Vaughan: "Crossfire"

SCRATCH RHYTHM

Scratch rhythm guitar is a ubiquitous effect that probably appears more on record than even in transcriptions. It basically refers to any time you strum a few or more strings while laying your fret hand lightly across them to create a muted, percussive effect. This sometimes happens unconsciously when moving between barre chords or power chords at fast tempos, but it's also one of the most important "non-tone" sounds that we create on the guitar. It can add depth and groove to your playing and help your rhythmic feel. It can even act as a well-placed hook in certain riffs.

One listen to players like Eddie Van Halen, Angus (or Malcom) Young, Steve Vai, Jimi Hendrix, and countless others will reveal the universal appeal of this technique. It's a huge part of the rock guitar sound, and many classic riffs would sound much less ballsy if it were absent.

Technical Talk

The concept behind the scratch rhythm is pretty simple. To hear what it sounds like, lay your fret-hand fingers lightly across all six strings (don't push them down to the fretboard) and strum the strings. Depending on how much gain you're using, it will sound thinner or thicker. Here's an example of the basic sound. Measure 1 is played with a clean tone, measure 2 is half dirty, and measure 3 is fully distorted.

Example 1

TRACK 53
:00

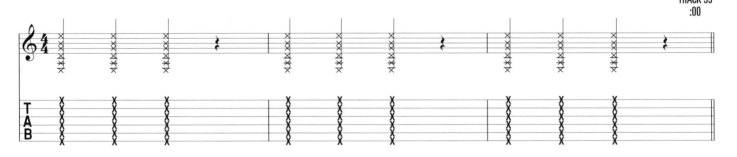

The sound will also vary slightly depending on where you're picking along the length of the string, just as the sound of normal notes will vary. In most instances, you'll probably be laying all four fingers on the strings to mute them. However, on certain phrases, you may have to experiment with certain fingers or combinations of fingers to get the desired effect.

Unintentional Harmonics

At extreme high gain settings, you'll most likely hear occasional high-pitched squeaks when using the technique. These are actually natural harmonics (see the Harmonics chapter) that are made more audible by the extreme gain and resulting compression. Many times, these end up sounding pretty cool, and players decide to leave them alone. If you don't want to hear them though, you'll need to adjust the position of your muting so that you're not producing a harmonic (or until you're producing a more pleasant harmonic anyway). Example 2 demonstrates this effect.

Example 2

TRACK 53
:13

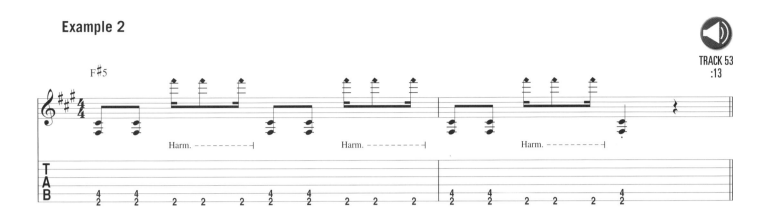

Exercises

Let's try some basic exercises to get used to the technique. The ability to seamlessly switch between standard fretting technique and scratch rhythm is what we're shooting for.

Example 3

TRACK 54
:00

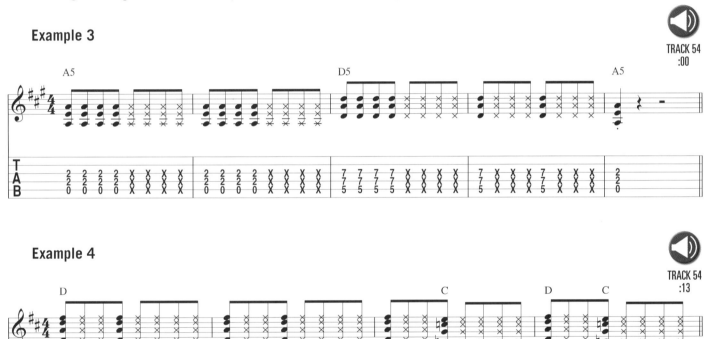

Example 4

TRACK 54
:13

In these final two exercises, we're working with sixteenth notes. You'll need to keep your fretting fingers in the same spot but just briefly release the pressure at the specified time.

Example 5

TRACK 54
:25

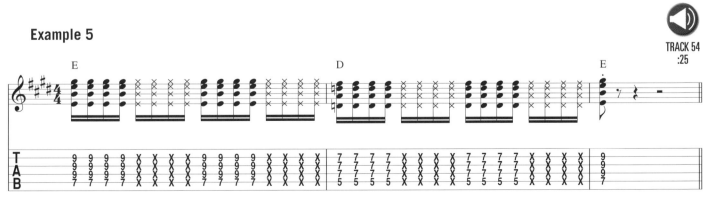

Example 6

TRACK 54
:37

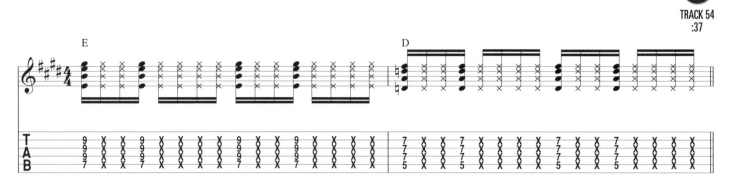

Riffs

Now let's put it to use in some typical riffs. The first one is classic hard rock guitar. You've heard this type of thing hundreds of times.

Example 7

TRACK 55
:00

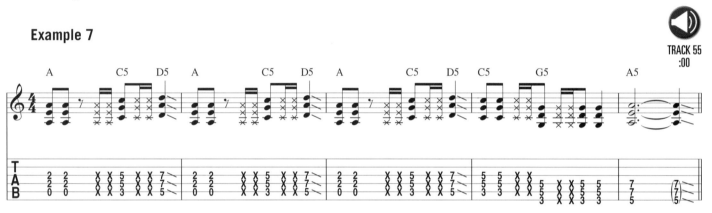

Here's one that's a bit funkier with sixteenth notes. We're using a cleaner tone here, so the scratches are a bit more subtle. They'd be very missed though if they weren't there.

Example 8

TRACK 55
:18

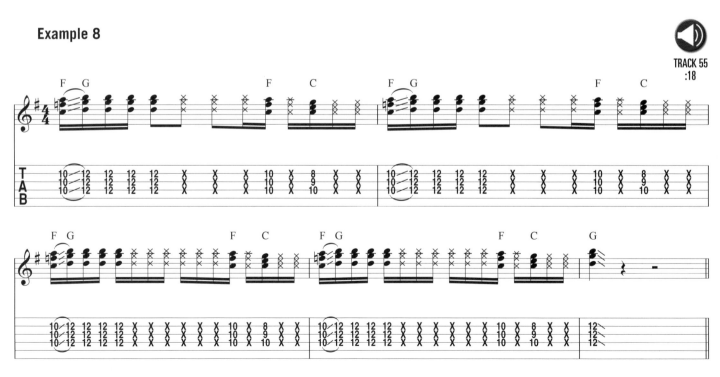

In this riff in A, we're exploiting the unintentional harmonics for maximum effect. Similar to the way the pitch of pinch harmonics isn't usually intentional, the harmonics produced don't really have to make sense to the key of the song. They're really more of a sound effect.

Example 9

TRACK 55
:33

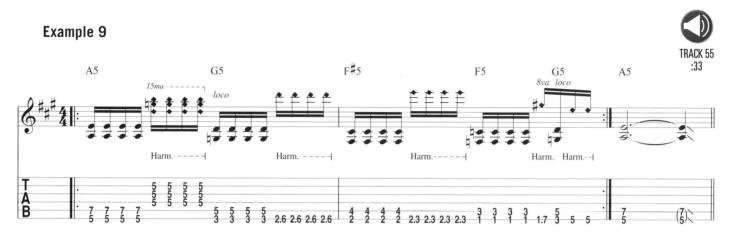

Here's an example that uses the scratch rhythm as the main hook of the riff. You'll hear this strategy often as well. It's kind of neat because a keyboardist can't really recreate it at all; this riff is all guitar!

Example 10

TRACK 55
:57

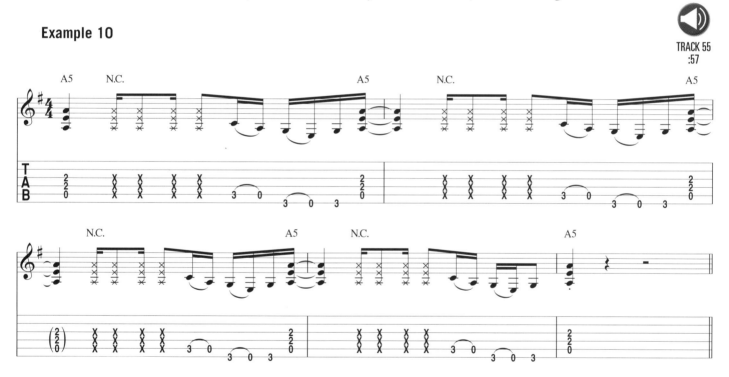

SUGGESTED LISTENING

Jimi Hendrix: "Machine Gun"

Van Halen: "You Really Got Me," "Cabo Wabo"

Steve Vai: "Bad Horsie"

Stevie Ray Vaughan: "Couldn't Stand the Weather"

Stone Temple Pilots: "Interstate Love Song"

Green Day: "Brain Stew"

SLIDE GUITAR

Many players never bother to mess with slide guitar, and it's a real shame in my opinion. Some of the most memorable riffs in rock history were played on slide, and it's an incredibly expressive tool that should be a part of every rock guitarist's arsenal. However, it requires a lot of practice to sound *really* good at it. Slide guitar is kind of like harmonica; there are those that have obviously devoted time to it, and then there are those that are just kind of faking it.

When you hear a true master of slide guitar like Derek Trucks, it's sometimes hard to believe what you're hearing. After all, he's (usually) playing every note by moving a single slide around. It's kind of like the equivalent of soloing with only one finger, although it's not quite that bad, because you don't have to push the strings down when you play slide. Nevertheless, developing Trucks' kind of facility is not an easy task.

The good news is that you don't have to become a virtuoso in order to appreciate the slide and exploit its unique tonal qualities. They're great for simple riffs as well, as we'll soon see. Many players develop a good, solid foundation on slide and keep it in their trick bag as an option for lending a different character to a song. And that's what we'll focus on here.

Technical Talk

Slides come in various shapes and are made from several different materials as well—the most common being glass or metal. Over the last decade, several products have become available that allow you to switch between slide playing and standard fretting without removing the slide. You should take some time to play with several different models to find one that suits you. Head to your local music store and try out everything they have available. Be sure to plug in if you plan to play on an electric guitar.

Basic Technique

Some players prefer to wear the slide on the pinky, some wear it on their third finger, and others wear it on their middle finger. There's no set rule on this (although, the index finger is rarely, if ever, used), so experiment to see what feels best. Each finger presents certain advantages and disadvantages. Wearing it on the pinky allows you to use your first three fingers for normal fretting when needed, but it limits your reach when doing so because you'll only be able to stretch from your index to your ring finger. Take your time in the beginning and find the slide finger that makes the most sense to you.

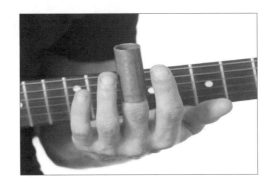

To play a note with the slide, we make contact with the string but don't push it down to the fretboard—similar to playing a natural harmonic (see Harmonics chapter). For proper tuning, you need to align the slide directly over the fretwire (also similar to natural harmonics). If you're out in front of the wire, you'll be sharp; if you're behind, you'll be flat.

After plucking the string, you can move the slide up or down to raise the pitch in a steady gliss.

Correct slide position for a note
on string 4, fret 5

Example 1

TRACK 56
:00

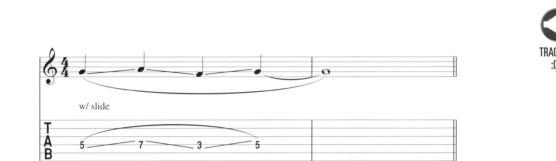

Muting

A very important part of clean slide playing is *muting*. This is accomplished by both hands working in conjunction with each other. On the fret hand, the fingers behind the slide should lightly touch all the strings to keep them quiet. This will prevent the other strings from making noise.

Regarding the pick hand, some players play slide with a pick, and others use fingerstyle or hybrid picking technique (see the Hybrid Picking chapter). Regardless of your preference, the pick-hand's job of muting is the same. You'll use your palm to mute all the bass strings below the string you're playing, just as when playing standard (see the Pick-Hand Muting chapter). That's the easy part. The tricky part is when you want to play only single notes with the slide on different strings and not allow them to ring together. In order to do this, you'll need to mute a string once you're not playing on it anymore. It's easiest to demonstrate with an example.

If I'm not concerned about keeping the notes separate, these two notes will ring together.

Example 2

TRACK 56
:12

However, if I want the notes to be separate, I'll need to mute the B string as soon as I pluck the G string. This is accomplished with a pick-hand finger.

Example 3

TRACK 56
:21

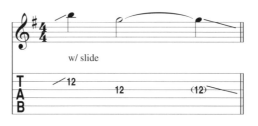

Because the slide acts like one big finger, it's always depressing the strings. So the separation of notes becomes the pick hand's responsibility. This will take some work at first, but it will eventually become second nature.

Open Tunings

Another aspect of slide guitar that can't be ignored is the open tuning. Ever since the days of Delta blues, guitarists have favored several open tunings for slide. Each one facilitates its own library of common slide licks and riffs, and again, there's not one established standard. Some players use open E or open D, some use open G, and some play slide in standard tuning. Here are the pitches for the most commonly employed open tunings.

- Open G: (low to high) D–G–D–G–B–D
- Open E: (low to high) E–B–E–G♯–B–E
- Open D: (low to high) D–A–D–F♯–A–D

(Note: Open E is the same tuning as open D, only all the strings are raised a whole step.)

Many players use standard tuning normally and then employ open tunings only when they play slide. Other players, such as Derek Trucks, Keith Richards, or Rich Robinson, use open tunings almost exclusively—with slide and without. Unless you learned from scratch to play in an open tuning, you'll most likely employ them only occasionally for slide playing. But, of course, feel free to experiment in this regard. You may find that an open tuning makes everything come together for you.

Exercises

Let's work on some slide fundamentals. All of these will be in standard tuning, though we'll explore some open tunings in the Licks section. This first one concentrates on playing in tune on all six strings. You may want to alternate using the slide and playing with standard technique to make sure you're matching the pitch.

Example 4

TRACK 57
:00

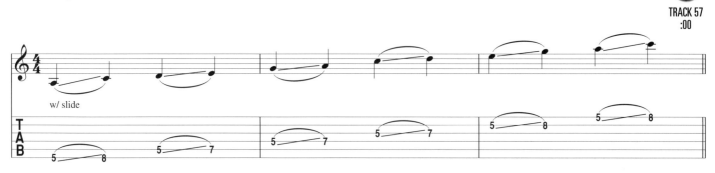

Here's an exercise that concentrates on another aspect of playing slide. In this example, we're allowing the A string to ring, so we need to keep the slide only on the upper strings.

Example 5

TRACK 57
:16

This example focuses on your pick-hand muting. If you're not using good muting technique, this one will sound pretty ugly. Alternating open strings with fretted notes like this is a prime condition for generating string noise. Do your best to keep it out!

Example 6

TRACK 57
:32

This final exercise focuses on sliding double stops. You have to be sure to keep the slide perpendicular to the neck so that both notes stay in tune.

Example 7

TRACK 57
:49

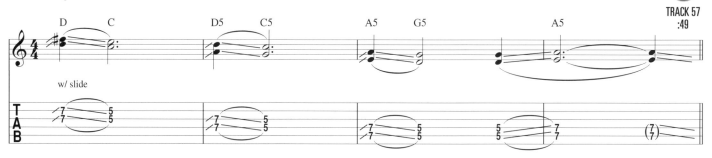

Licks

Standard Tuning

Our first standard tuned lick uses the G minor pentatonic scale and will require a good pick-hand muting technique. Make sure none of the notes are bleeding together.

Example 8

TRACK 58
:00

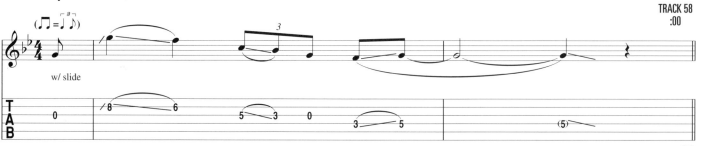

Here's one in E major that's reminiscent of George Harrison's slide work. This one's going for a straight sound as opposed to the bluesier sound that's typical with slide work. Also, notice that we're adding vibrato to the last note. To add vibrato with the slide, simply volley the slide back and fourth, surround the target pitch to create an average "in tune" note.

Example 9

TRACK 58
:09

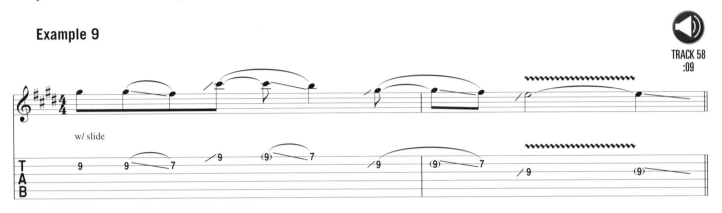

Here's a lick in G that makes use of some triple stops for a thicker sound. You may have noticed earlier that, in open G tuning, strings 4, 3, and 2 are the same pitch as in standard tuning. We're exploiting that fact here to mimic an open G slide riff.

Example 10

TRACK 58
:17

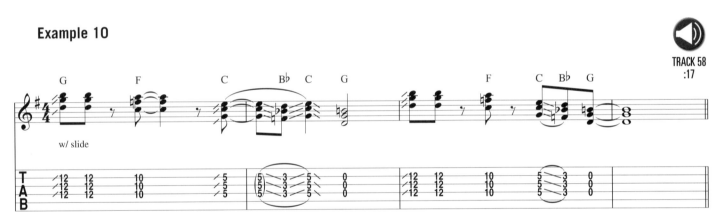

Open G

Now let's take a look at some open G licks. From standard tuning, you'll need to lower your sixth string down a whole step to D, lower your fifth string down a whole step to G, and lower your first string down a whole step to D. Here's a typical open G line that makes use of open strings—a very common practice in any open tuning.

Example 11

TRACK 59
:00

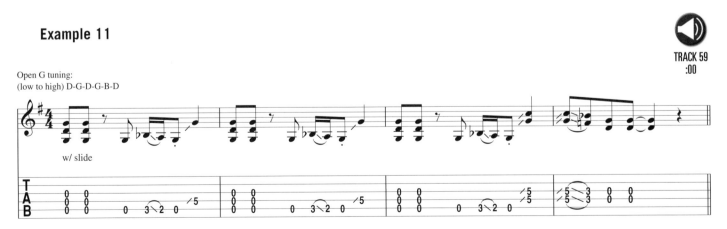

Obviously, most people play in the key of G while in open G tuning. Here's a nice syncopated riff in the style of Rich Robinson.

Example 12

TRACK 59
:14

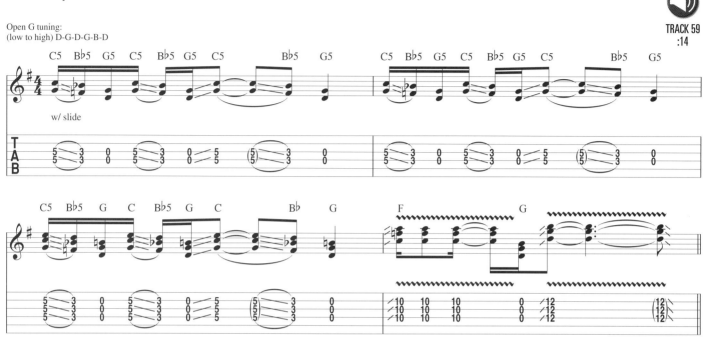

This final open G lick covers all six strings at one point. Watch the pick-hand muting!

Example 13

TRACK 59
:29

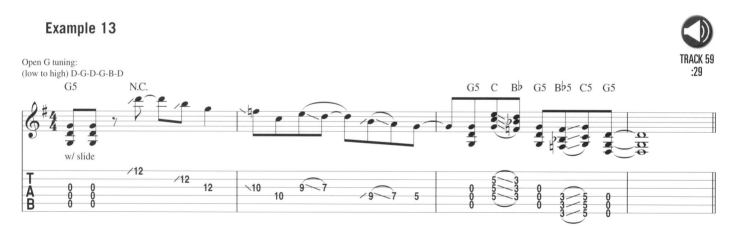

Open D

We'll close out with some licks in open D. Remember that any lick you learn in open D can also be used in open E; it will just sound a whole step higher. This first one is a classic in the style of Duane Allman.

Example 14

TRACK 60
:00

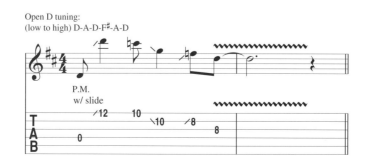

Here's one that exploits the octave D strings for a thick, full melody.

Example 15

This final lick works on several aspects we've covered: double stops, pick-hand muting, and open strings.

Example 16

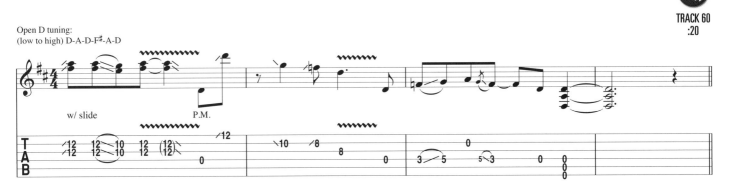

SUGGESTED LISTENING

Joe Walsh: "Life's Been Good"

Black Crowes: "Twice as Hard"

Jimi Hendrix: "All Along the Watchtower"

Tesla: "Heaven's Trail (No Way Out)"

The Allman Brothers Band: "Statesboro Blues"

STRING SKIPPING

If you feel you've hit a rut and keep playing the same old licks over and over, you should check out string skipping. The technique has been adopted and assimilated by some stellar players—including Eric Johnson, Paul Gilbert, Steve Vai, and Allan Holdsworth to name a few—to create some colorful, ear-grabbing, wide-interval phrases that always inject excitement into a solo.

The cool thing about the technique is that you can start to apply it almost immediately just by re-thinking how you approach your scale patterns. Even a minor pentatonic scale can sound new again with a bit of string skipping. You can create traditional, classical-sounding phrases or get as far out as you want with it. One thing is for sure; you're guaranteed to have some fun.

Technical Talk

A string skipping lick is simply one that involves some notes played on non-adjacent strings. You're "skipping" over a string (or two or three or more) to play notes on a higher (or lower) string. This can be done in a very formulaic fashion similar to Paul Gilbert, or it can be a bit more off the cuff and unpredictable-sounding in the vein of Eric Johnson or Allan Holdsworth. Let's look at how to get started.

The Basic Idea

We can begin very simply to illustrate the concept. Let's take the typical A minor pentatonic scale in fifth position. If we ascend straight up through the scale, it sounds as typical as an A5 chord.

Example 1

TRACK 61
:00

But now, let's apply some string skipping to create a more interesting sound. We'll play exactly the same notes, but we'll just jumble up the order of the strings a bit.

Example 2

TRACK 61
:07

All of a sudden it catches your ear, huh? You can apply this idea to any scale pattern to get new sounds. Here's the same type of thing applied to a C major scale arranged in three notes per string.

Example 3

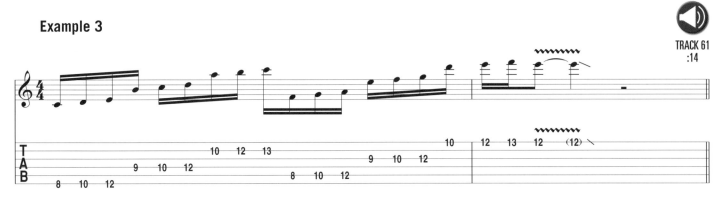

TRACK 61
:14

You're really only bound by your imagination with this type of thing.

Picking Concerns

Once you've dabbled with this, you'll no doubt notice that some picking maneuvers are quite tricky to pull off at high speeds. The move from a downstroke on string 2 to an upstroke on string 5 in Example 3 is a good example of this. Therefore, players often mix in legato moves if necessary to make the skips less awkward. In the above scenario, for example, you may choose to use a hammer-on from B to C on string 2 (or for all three notes: A–B–C), which will allow you time to get the pick ready on string 5. At that point, you could continue the line on string 5 with an upstroke or choose to start with a downstroke.

Exercises

Let's do some exercises to get a feel for this. This first one concentrates mostly on the right hand picking, using only frets 5 and 7 throughout. Technically, these notes all fall within the A Dorian mode, so you could use it that way, but our main focus is making sure the picking is clean and accurate.

Example 4

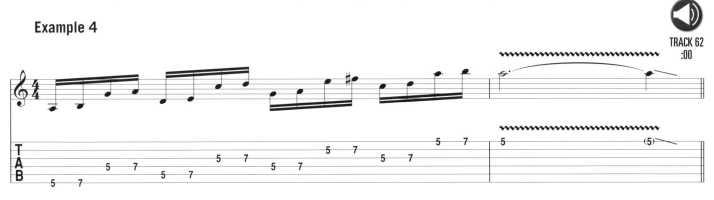

TRACK 62
:00

And here's a descending idea that uses three-note groups on each string: frets 8, 7, and 5 for each. Again, the focus here is on the picking.

Example 5

TRACK 62
:09

Here's an interesting exercise that uses two adjacent strings and two more with a string skipped between the pair. It's a very unique picking motion and will probably take a bit to work up. I'm using straight alternate picking here, but feel free to experiment in this regard.

Example 6

TRACK 62
:17

And here's a colorful-sounding exercise that skips constantly, descending and ascending. This one's a real bear on the pick hand.

Example 7

TRACK 62
:31

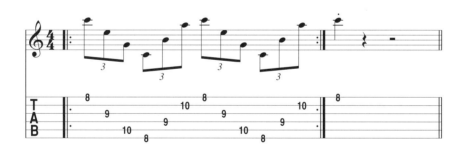

Licks

Ok, let's try this technique out on some fresh-sounding licks. Our first is a Paul Gilbert-inspired run in D major that works on the 1/3 string pair and then the 4/2 pair. Try this one as written and also experiment with legato moves in different spots.

Example 8

TRACK 63
:00

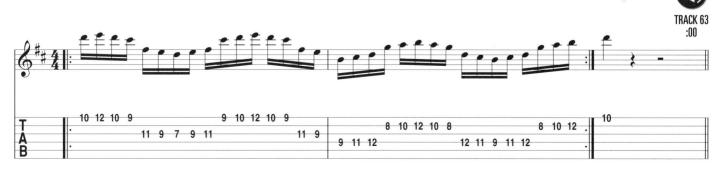

Here's one that sounds a bit like something Allan Holdsworth would do. The wide stretches and legato feel are staples of the Holdsworth sound.

Example 9

TRACK 63
:28

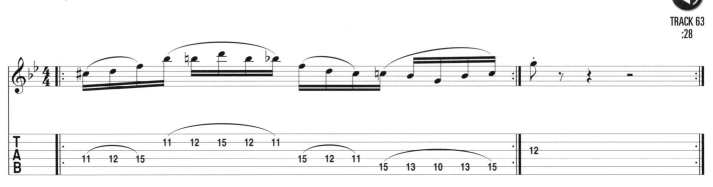

Example 10 is an Eric Johnson-inspired line in D minor that mixes some standard box playing with some wide-interval surprises. Though the tempo isn't too fast here, the thirty-second notes get a little speedy.

Example 10

TRACK 63
:43

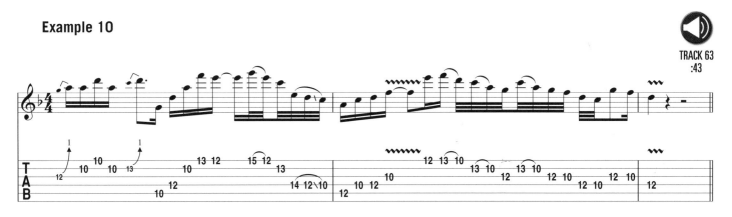

Here's a fusion-sounding lick in Bb that's a bit more free-form in its string skipping. There's really not a pattern at work here. It's more about jumbling up notes in an interesting way at one spot on the fretboard.

Example 11

TRACK 64
:00

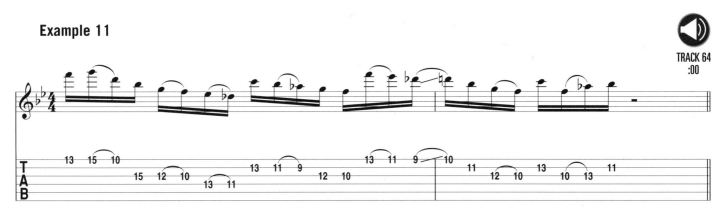

This phrase takes a page out of the Eric Johnson playbook. We're arpeggiating through several open-voiced triads in the key of A—something that became widely emulated after Johnson's groundbreaking *Ah Via Musicom* album.

Example 12

TRACK 64
:15

This final lick is a colorful phrase in C minor that makes use of the C minor hexatonic scale (C–D–E♭–F–G–B♭). It's also slightly reminiscent of Eric Johnson in the beginning, but it settles into an interesting pattern for the descent.

Example 13

TRACK 64
:34

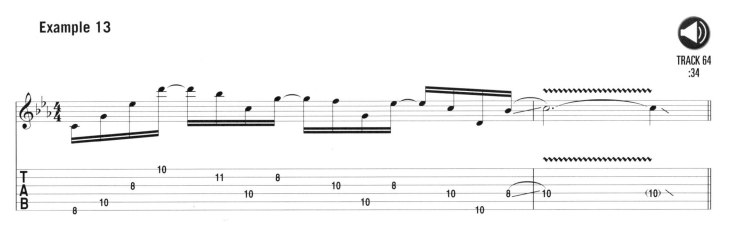

SUGGESTED LISTENING

Eric Johnson: "Cliffs of Dover," "Desert Rose," "Camel's Night Out"

Allan Holdsworth: "Devil Take the Hindmost," "Metal Fatigue"

Extreme: "Get the Funk Out"

Racer X: "Poison Eyes"

Steve Morse: "Tumeni Notes"

SWEEP PICKING

Ah, sweep picking. Not since tapping has a technique lured so many would-be shredders with its promise of flash. The truth is that, while nearly every shredder has dabbled with it, few have truly mastered it. It's a difficult technique and not something that can be picked up over an extended weekend practice session. If you're totally new to the technique, there are several aspects that may feel extremely awkward at first. It's only through careful, controlled practice that sweep picking will begin to fall under your fingers.

To hear what this technique can sound like when mastered, check out Yngwie Malmsteen, Jason Becker, Frank Gambale (for a fusion slant), and George Bellas, although there are many other brilliant sweepers. It's a technique that allows the guitarist to play things otherwise impossible with alternate picking (at the same speed, anyway). But be careful; it can sound amazingly fluid when done cleanly, but it can sound extremely ugly otherwise!

Technical Talk

The basic idea with sweep picking is that you're either ascending or descending through the strings one at a time with one continuous pick stroke. This is most commonly applied to arpeggios, but we'll see in the licks section that other sweeps are possible as well. So instead of using alternate picking to play the following line, you'd use one continuous downstroke.

Example 1

TRACK 65
:00

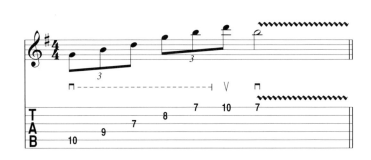

There are several things that all have to happen simultaneously in order for this to sound clean and fluid at higher tempos. Let's look at those now.

Synchronization

One of the most important elements in sweep picking is that your picking hand and fret hand be perfectly in sync with each other. If one gets ahead or behind, either a note is going to get clipped or bleed into another. Either one of these will destroy the fluidity of the line. Developing this synchronization comes with hours and hours of practice with a metronome. Start extremely slowly and work up the speed gradually.

Pick-Hand Muting

Another important aspect of clean sweep picking is the muting of the bass strings by the pick hand. Any time you're picking string 2, your palm should be following along by muting strings 3–6. When you reach string 1, your palm should be muting strings 2–6, and so on. This needs to become automatic. The problem with this is that it's a different motion if you've only been familiar with alternate picking. Sweeping requires some forearm movement, which will feel awkward at first. With practice, though, you'll get a feel for it.

Fret-Hand Technique

The fret hand has to be extremely precise as well. Even though you'll be sweeping through chord shapes, you don't want them to sound like a chord. You want them to sound like a single-note arpeggio. This means that one finger needs to get off a note as soon as the next one is on another. However, that's not the only problem. Many sweeping shapes require you to roll a finger across two strings on the same fret—and sometimes three. This motion is very difficult to pull off without bleeding the notes together. And it's something that needs to be learned in both ascending and descending forms, because each requires a slightly different technique. Again, slow and steady practice is the name of the game here.

Exercises

Ok, let's get to some exercises that concentrate on the fundamentals. Examples 2–6 work on three- and four-string sweeps on major and minor arpeggios, ascending and descending. Work these up slowly and make sure you're only hearing one note at a time. The last minor form in Example 5 is very difficult to play cleanly. You'll really have to be precise when rolling your index finger.

Example 2

TRACK 65
:09

Example 3

TRACK 65
:27

Example 4

TRACK 65
:44

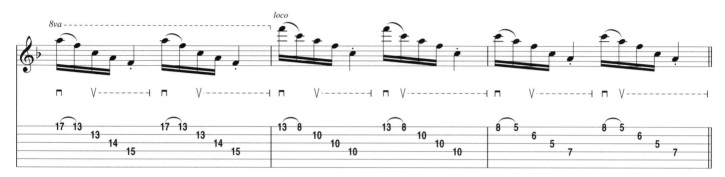

Example 5

TRACK 65
1:02

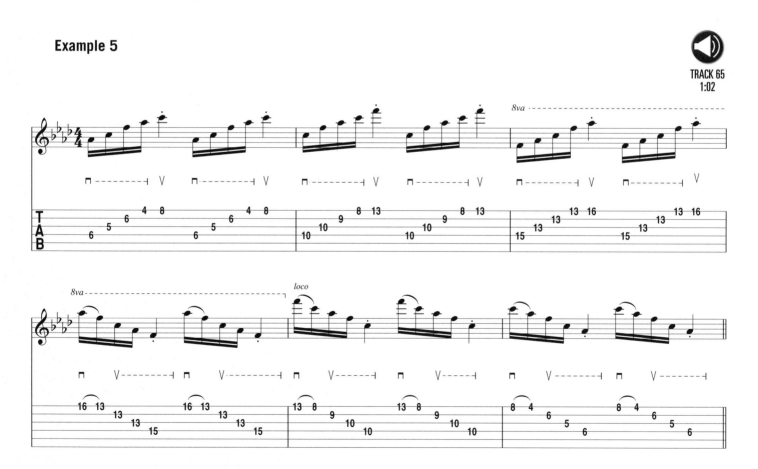

Examples 6–9 work on five- and six-string major and minor arpeggio shapes. Note where the hammer-ons and pull-offs are and pay close attention to the picking directions.

Example 6

TRACK 66
:00

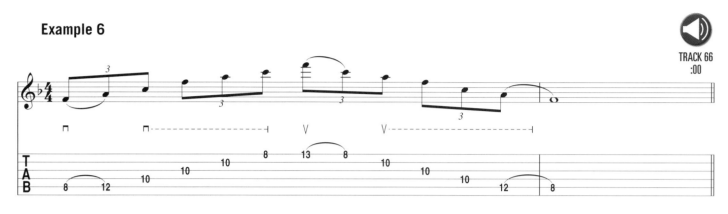

Example 7

TRACK 66
:10

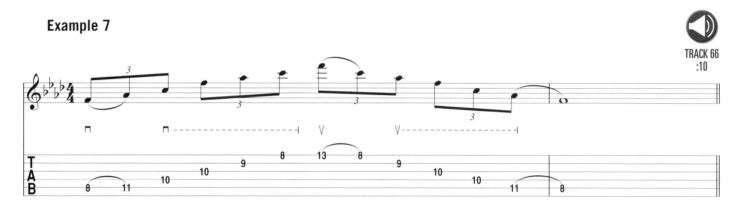

Example 8

TRACK 66
:18

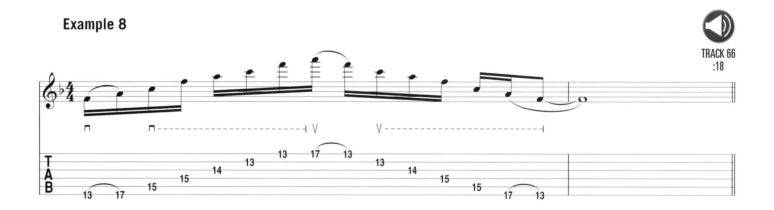

Example 9

TRACK 66
:27

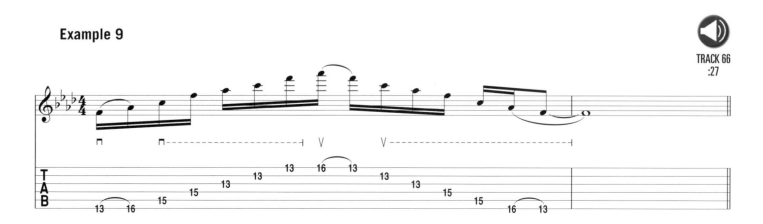

Example 10 is a spider-finger exercise that sounds demented but really helps with synchronizing the hands. Begin this one very slowly and work it up to tempo gradually.

Example 10

TRACK 66
:36

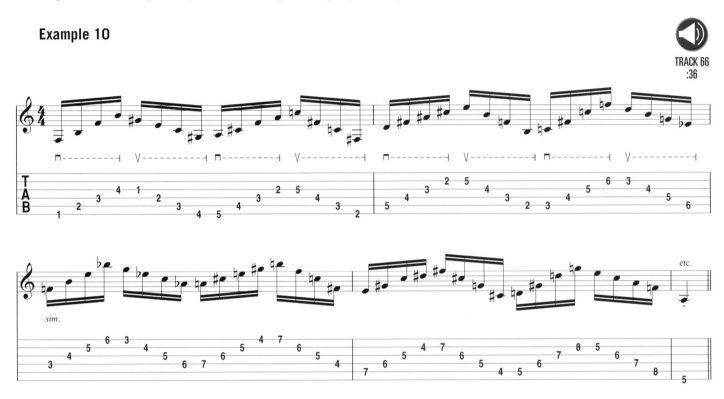

Licks

Now on to the licks. This first one is a classic sweeping pattern in A minor on the top three strings.

Example 11

TRACK 67
:00

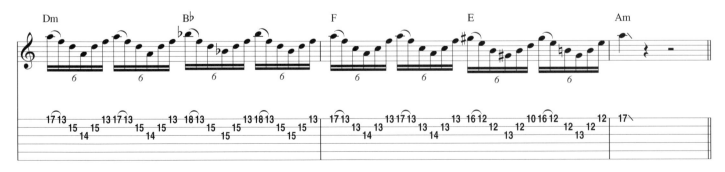

Here's another typical pattern using five-string shapes. We're working through a i–♭VII–♭VI–V progression in C minor.

Example 12

TRACK 67
:39

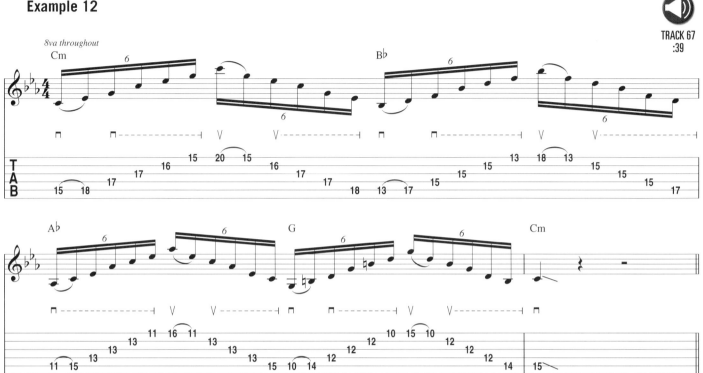

In this lick, we begin with another common pattern on the treble strings, but then we move into a few less common shapes and mix up the sweeps with some legato moves to outline a Gm7–C7 progression that resolves to F on the final note.

Example 13

TRACK 67
1:05

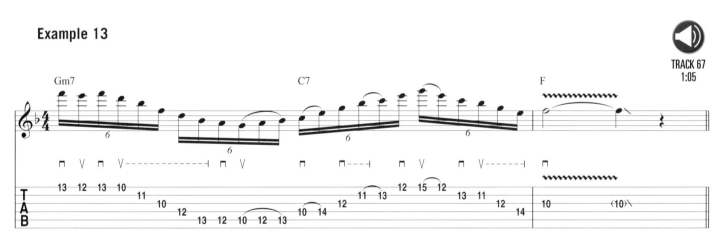

For this final lick, we begin by sweeping up a colorful Cmaj6/9 shape, which is not very common but sounds great. We continue by tonicizing E minor with a G–B7 sweep and finish off with a multi-octave E minor sweep.

Example 14

TRACK 67
1:23

SUGGESTED LISTENING

Yngwie Malmsteen: "Black Star"

Jason Becker: "Altitudes"

Frank Gambale: "Frankly Speaking," "Duet Tuet"

Dream Theater: "The Glass Prison"

TAPPING

The two-handed tapping technique is pretty much the holy grail of flashy technique. Never before had guitarists been able to produce such a blur of notes. Though he wasn't the first to do it (you can find instances of tapping that date back to the sixties), the popularization of the technique is unquestionably credited to Eddie Van Halen. With the release of *Van Halen* in 1978, the whole world of rock guitar shook as the jaws of every player on the planet hit the floor. Part of what made the album such a monumental debut is that Eddie hadn't just been tinkering with the technique at the time of the release; he had fully mastered it. And, quite simply, it blew everyone's minds—the way Hendrix had done over a decade earlier.

As the eighties progressed, many other players, such as Steve Vai, Joe Satriani, Reb Beach, and Vito Bratta, adapted the technique and created a massive library of tapping techniques that continues to expand today. In the minds of many players, however, Eddie is still the tapping king.

Technical Talk

Tapping is a legato technique whereby the first (or second) finger of the pick hand is basically treated as an extra fret-hand digit with which one can hammer on and pull off notes. It's quite ingenious in its simplicity, and it enables players to blaze through arpeggios on a single string quite possibly faster than any other instrument. Unlike tapped harmonics (see Harmonics chapter), with tapping you do want to press the string all the way down to the fret board.

Let's look at the basic technique. Since some players prefer to tap with their first finger and others use their second, I'm simply going to refer to your "tapping finger" throughout this chapter. In Example 1, tap onto fret 12 of the third string and then pull off to the seventh fret, which should be fretted with the fret hand.

Example 1

TRACK 68
:00

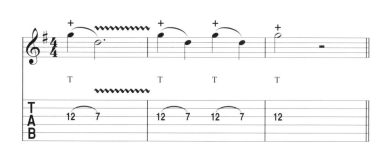

That's the basic idea, although there are several things you need to keep in mind if you want to achieve a clean sound. Let's examine more closely.

Tapping Precision

You need to make sure that you're not nudging any adjacent strings when you tap onto the note, as this will cause unwanted string noise and/or extraneous notes. Most players brace their tapping hand by holding the top of the neck with their thumb. This provides a good bit of stability and makes it a bit easier to hit your target.

Bracing tapping hand with thumb on top of neck

Muting lower strings with palm of tapping hand

Muting

You'll also want to employ good muting technique with both hands to prevent unwanted noises from creeping into your lines. Use the palm of your tapping hand to lightly touch the bass strings when you're not playing them. The treble strings—the E and B strings when you're playing the G string, for example—can usually be kept quiet by the underside of the fret-hand's first finger.

Exercises

Let's work on the basics with some exercises before we tackle some licks.

Single String

Examples 2–5 work on tapping one string at a time while adding more fret-hand fingers into the mix. Remember to listen closely and make sure no extraneous noise is popping out.

Example 2

TRACK 68
:12

Example 3

TRACK 68
:20

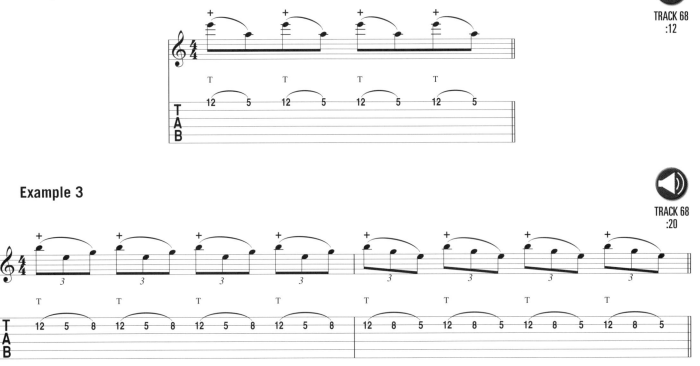

Example 4

TRACK 68
:30

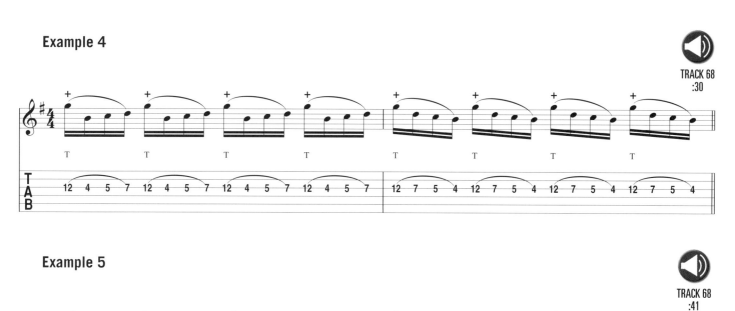

Example 5

TRACK 68
:41

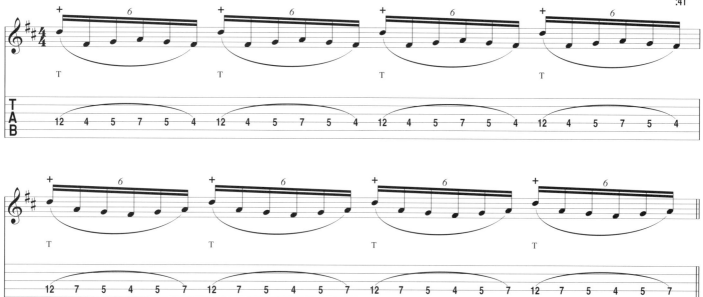

Moving Through Strings

Now let's work on moving up and down through the strings. We're using symmetrical fingerings here so we can focus on the tapping technique, but when we tackle the actual licks, we'll be conforming our hands to scale patterns, which will require some practice.

Example 6

TRACK 69
:00

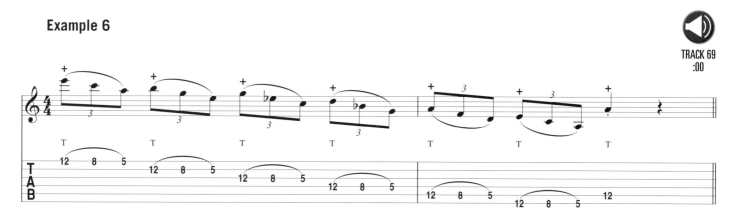

Example 7

TRACK 69
:09

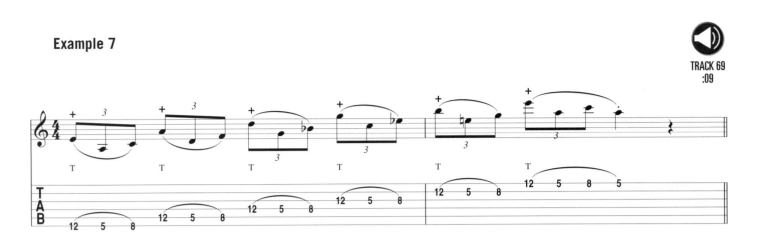

Example 8

TRACK 69
:17

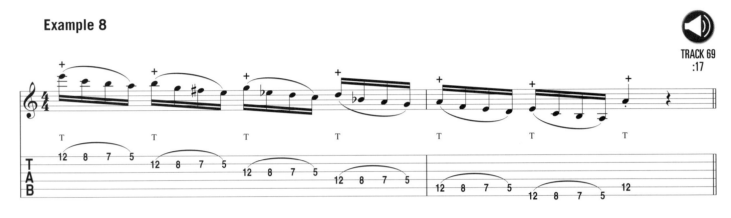

Example 9

TRACK 69
:25

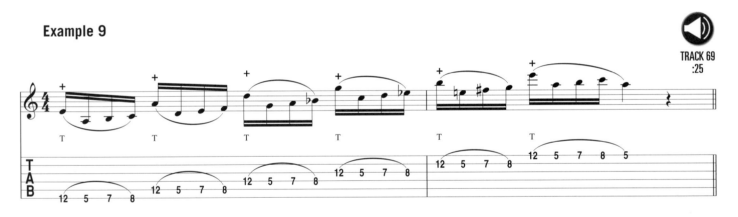

Licks

Ok let's get to the licks. Here's a typical one-string move with tapping: keeping either the fret hand in the same place and moving the tapping finger or vice versa. This E minor lick uses both concepts.

Example 10

TRACK 70
:00

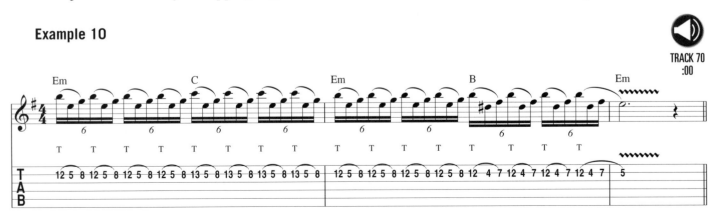

This next lick is a descending phrase that uses four-note groups on strings 1–4. We finish off by tapping the low E string at the twelfth fret and adding vibrato. To add vibrato to a tapped note, you use your fret hand. The tapped finger simply holds on for the ride.

Example 11

TRACK 70
:25

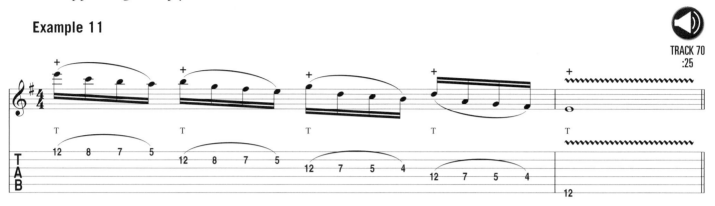

Here's another common tapping concept: doubling up on the tapped note to create a sextuplet phrase. In this lick, we move this idea up through the strings. We end by bending a tapped note up to the tonic C. As with vibrato, the bend is executed by the fretting hand; the tapping finger just holds on.

Example 12

TRACK 70
:37

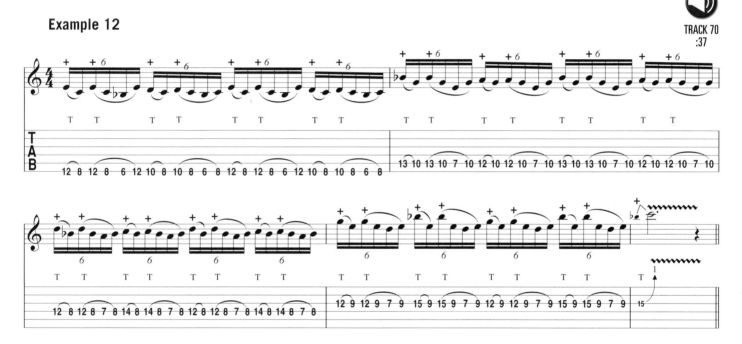

In Example 13, we fully explore the tapped bend technique. To sound the first bend, simply pluck the string with the tapping finger near the twelfth fret so you'll be ready to tap right away. While holding the seventh-fret bend, tap the twelfth fret (which will now sound an A note instead of G) and pull off. Then release the bend and continue with the pull-offs to the open G string. For the final A note in beat 2, use a "hammer-on from nowhere" (see the Legato chapter).

Example 13

TRACK 71
:00

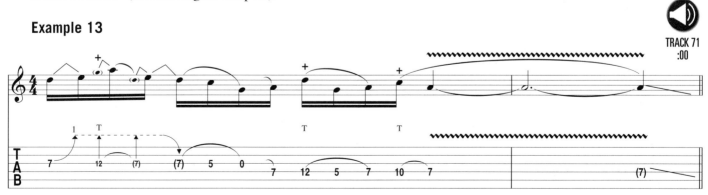

And here's another option with tapping: the *tapped slide*. We're remaining on the B string for this E blues lick. The tapped slide is pretty self-explanatory; just tap the note and slide your tapping finger up and down a half step before pulling off. Be sure to maintain solid pressure on the string so the notes are clear.

Example 14

TRACK 71
:18

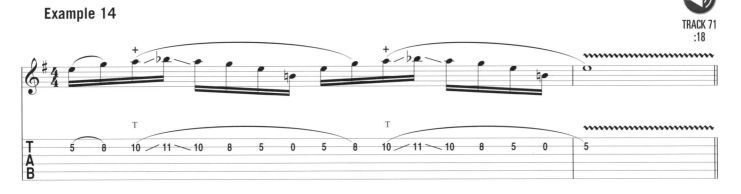

Here's a cool descending sequence using the B minor pentatonic scale that makes use of hammer-ons from nowhere each time we move down a string. Be sure none of the notes are bleeding into each other.

Example 15

TRACK 71
:34

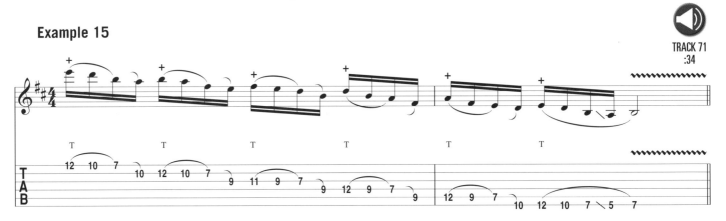

For our final lick, we're combining all these techniques into one lick using the C blues scale. Take it slow and make sure it's clean.

Example 16

TRACK 71
:49

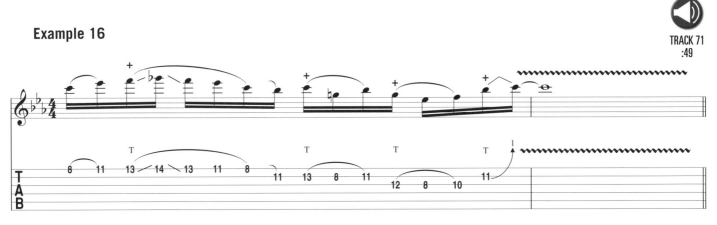

SUGGESTED LISTENING

Van Halen: "Eruption," "Hot for Teacher," "Source of Infection"

Joe Satriani: "Satch Boogie," "Always with Me, Always with You"

Mr. Big: "Addicted to That Rush"

Steve Vai: "Bad Horsie," "Big Trouble" (with David Lee Roth)

TOGGLE SWITCH STUTTER EFFECT

Also called the "machine gun effect," "kill switch trick," and other colorful terms, the toggle switch stutter is an ultra-cool effect that can create an otherworldly sound without any additional equipment needed. The only prerequisite is that you have a guitar with Gibson-style wiring. This includes (typically) a three-way pickup selector switch and independent volume controls for both pickups. It's a whole lot of fun to pull this one off and watch the audience's eyes light up in amazement.

Technical Talk

To set up this move, you simply need to turn one volume up (all the way for the most prominent effect) and turn the other volume all the way down. If you're playing on the bridge pickup, for example, turn it all the way up and make sure the neck pickup's volume is completely off. Crank up the gain, strike a chord (or a note), and then flick the toggle switch back and forth between the middle and bridge positions. The chord will stutter in the rhythm of your toggle switch manipulation. It's common to use a good amount of reverb or some ambient delay when performing this move.

It should be noted that, if you make extensive use of this trick, your toggle switch may eventually malfunction. This is especially common if the guitar is an inexpensive model, where they keep the price down by implementing lower quality electronics and less-than-stellar quality control. If the solder joints in your toggle switch are at all subject, repeatedly performing this trick will probably cause the switch to eventually fail. The good news is that, if you're decent with a soldering iron (and it's not hard to learn at all), this is an easy fix, and a quality repair should be able to stand up to the maneuver for probably the life of the instrument.

Licks

Let's hear how this bit of guitar magic sounds. Example 1 is a typical application: a big, fat A5 chord that trails off in stuttering fashion.

Example 1

TRACK 72
:00

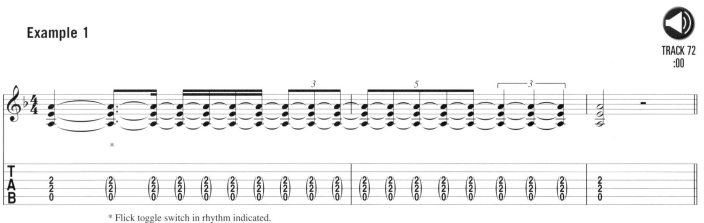

* Flick toggle switch in rhythm indicated.

And here's another great effect: the falling bend. After plucking the bent note, gradually release it while toggling the switch back and forth.

Example 2

TRACK 72
:13

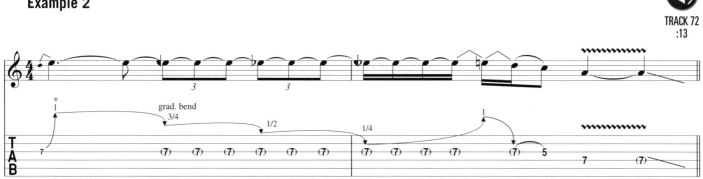

* Gradually release bend while flicking toggle switch in rhythm indicated.

This next lick uses the "hammer-on from nowhere" technique (see the Legato chapter) to sound every note. If you use a good amount of gain, you can simply hammer on to the string forcefully and still sound a good, solid note—no pick needed. (This is easiest on the lower strings, but still possible on the treble ones too.) This frees up your pick hand to operate the toggle switch. You can begin with it in the off position and flick it on each time you hammer a new note for a robotic, synthesized effect. You'll need to employ a good amount of fret-hand muting as well to keep the notes clear (see the Fret-Hand Muting chapter).

Example 3

TRACK 73
:00

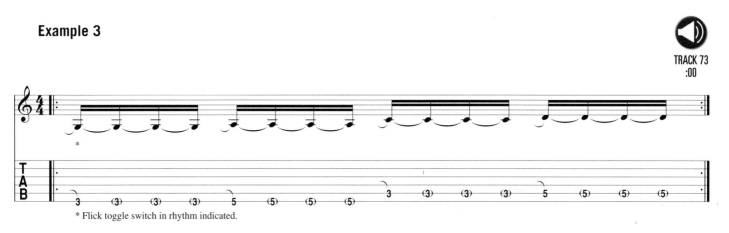

* Flick toggle switch in rhythm indicated.

This final lick expands on the previous idea with the use of a delay effect. Set the delay for a single repeat at a dotted eighth note. When you play eighth notes using the technique described in Example 3, the delayed notes will fall in between, creating a sixteenth-note line.

Example 4

TRACK 74

* Hammer on w/ fret hand and flick toggle switch to sound notes.
** Set for dotted 8th note w/ one repeat.

SUGGESTED LISTENING

Van Halen: "You Really Got Me"

Rage Against the Machine: "Bulls on Parade"

Ozzy Osbourne: "Crazy Train (live version)"

Sweet: "Fox on the Run"

The Pretenders: "Tattooed Love Boys"

TREMOLO PICKING

Tremolo picking is often associated with intensity and putting the pedal to the metal for the climax of an extended solo, but it's not a one trick pony by any means. It can also be used to provide feathery mandolin-style flourishes or provide the melodic backbone to a surf tune. Sure, in the hands of someone like Stevie Ray Vaughan, it could be used to grind the audience into a pulp of submission, but it does have a softer, more controlled side. We'll examine all of its facets here.

Technical Talk

The concept of tremolo picking is fairly simple: you simply pick a note (or notes) as fast as you possibly can. Just as with standard picking technique, there's not one set standard motion that players use for tremolo picking. Many players even use a different picking technique when they tremolo pick, such as Eddie Van Halen, who arches his wrist away from the guitar and flutters his wrist rapidly. Again, there are those that maintain you must tremolo pick the way you normally pick, but there are just too many examples that prove this not to be true.

You'll need to experiment to see which motion feels natural to you. You may even use different motions depending on the effect you're going for. If you're tremolo picking a triple stop with reckless abandon, you may find that you'll put your whole forearm into it. If you're picking a soft melody mandolin-style, you may find that the motion will all come from the wrist. Or maybe exactly the opposite will work best for you.

Precision

Whichever method you choose, you'll need to be precise and controlled about it if you want to ever tremolo pick a melody on any of the inner strings. (The outer E strings are a bit easier, since you have a bit more pick room.) Try to remain relaxed, and don't hold your breath. There may be times when you'll need to continue the technique for an extended period of time, and tensing up and/or holding your breath will make that difficult. Try to visualize an even, steady flow of motion and allow your hands to do what's needed to make that happen.

Muting

During those times when calm precision is not what you're shooting for, there are other concerns. If you're "mowing the lawn"—i.e., tremolo picking double- or triple-stops with reckless abandon—during a high-energy solo, you're going to need to employ some fret-hand muting in order to keep surrounding open strings from joining the fray (see the Fret-Hand Muting chapter). When you're playing that intensely, you don't want to have to worry about picking only two or three strings at a time. It will actually sound beefier if you can include a few muted strings in your strumming, anyway.

Licks

Let's hear how the technique sounds in some various applications. This first lick is a melody played entirely on the G string with one finger sliding to every note. This is a common application of the tremolo technique.

Example 1

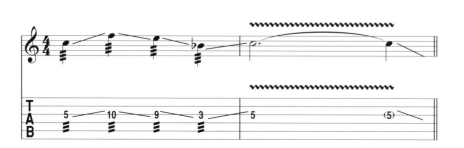

TRACK 75
:00

In this lick, we're still playing a single-note melody, but we're moving through several strings. This will take a bit of getting used to, but it's not as troublesome as it might first appear.

Example 2

TRACK 75
:11

Here's a more raucous example using double stops. Notice also that we're re-attacking them with slides for added effect. Be sure to use fret-hand muting here.

Example 3

TRACK 76
:00

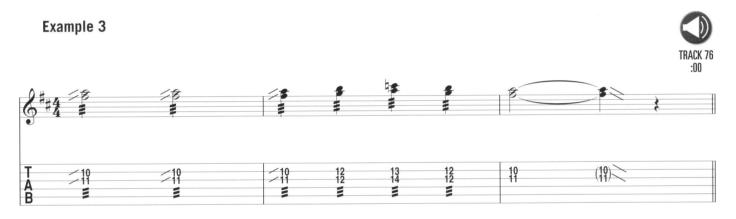

Here's another common idea: 6ths or octaves on non-adjacent strings. In this lick, we're using both. You have no choice but to use fret-hand muting here to keep the in-between string quiet.

Example 4

TRACK 76
:13

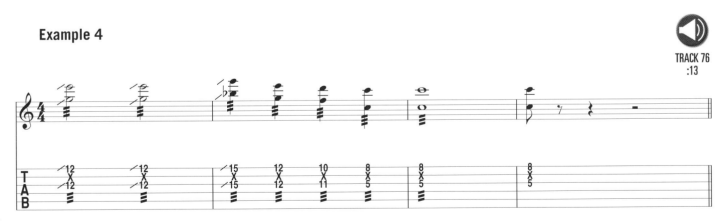

This final lick is the classic "tremolo-picked final chord of the night." The drummer's going crazy, and you're bashing out this chord, waiting for him to finish his super-extended final drum fill.

Example 5

TRACK 76
:26

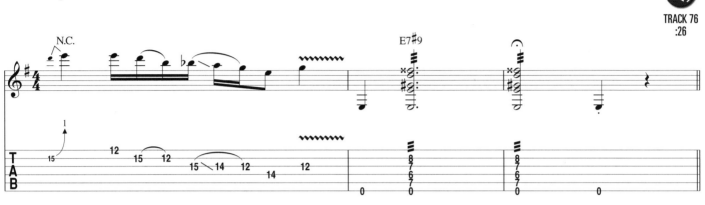

SUGGESTED LISTENING

The Chantays: "Pipeline"

Dick Dale: "Misirlou"

Steve Vai: "The Riddle"

Van Halen: "Eruption"

Stevie Ray Vaughan: "Texas Flood" (*Live at El Mocambo* version)

TRILLS

Once the signature of Baroque melodies, the trill—the rapid fluctuation of two pitches—has been adopted by blues and rock guitarists and put to good use throughout the years. It can be flashy or understated, and it's not easy, though Hendrix, Stevie Ray, and many others make it look that way. You'll need a solid legato technique (see the Legato chapter) and a good bit of endurance too. You'll feel the burn in your forearm for sure!

Technical Talk

On the guitar, we perform trills by stringing hammer-ons and pull-offs together continuously. Usually, the lower note is picked once, which is almost always fretted by the first finger (unless it's an open string), and then a higher note is hammered on, pulled off, hammered on, pulled off, ad infinitum as quickly as possible. Trills of a whole step or half step are most common, although larger intervals are used as well. Here's the basic idea on the D string.

Example 1

TRACK 77
:00

Trills with open strings are also quite common.

Example 2

TRACK 77
:09

Trills do not come easily. If you've never worked on them before, don't expect to be blurring through them the way Stevie Ray or Hendrix did. Your arm is going to get tired, so be sure to rest if you feel any pain.

TRILLING WITH EVERY FINGER?

In many technique books, you'll find many people state that you should practice trilling with every finger combination possible—i.e., trilling not only with 1 and 2, 1 and 3, and 1 and 4, but also with 2 and 3, 2 and 4, and 3 and 4. While this may be ideal in a perfect world, I can't say that I've ever seen a rock guitarist trilling with the second or the third finger as the base note as well as they can with the first finger. If you want to knock yourself out though with this, feel free!

Tapped Trills

A variation on the technique is the *tapped trill*. Here, instead of using a fret-hand finger to hammer on and pull off, you use your tapping finger (see the Tapping chapter). This is a nice option to have because it can save your left hand from turning to jelly if you need to trill for an extended period of time.

Many players, such as Joe Satriani, use their pick to tap with when performing a tapped trill. This provides a different tone, and it can produce a faster trill because less motion is required.

Example 3

TRACK 78
:00

Alternating Tapped Trills

Yet another possible trill technique is to alternate a fret-hand finger with your tapping finger. In other words, you pick the note, hammer and pull off with your fret hand, and then tap and pull off the same fret with your tapping finger.

It gets a little cramped up on the higher frets, but it's still doable. This method allows for the fastest trilling by far with half the physical effort of the standard or tapped trill.

Example 4

TRACK 78
:09

* Alternate hammering w/ fret hand
and tapping for trill.

Exercises

Here are a few exercises to help build a strong trill. Try to make sure the notes are all clear, and be sure to move these exercises to different strings and different areas on the neck. It doesn't feel the same at all trilling on the first fret as it does on the fifteenth.

Example 5

TRACK 79
:00

Example 6

TRACK 79
:14

Example 7

TRACK 79
:29

* Trill by tapping with edge of pick throughout.

Licks

Our first lick is a blues rock staple and involves playing an A7 triple stop and trilling on the middle string. Trilling from the minor to major 3rd of a chord is a classic move.

Example 8

TRACK 80
:00

And here's another bluesy move that's been used by everyone from Hendrix to Eddie Van Halen to Joe Satriani.

Example 9

TRACK 80
:15

This next lick is something else that Hendrix would do occasionally. You're performing a continuous trill on the G string while moving to different areas of the neck. Notice that the trill varies between whole steps and half steps in order to conform to the notes of the key—E Dorian in this case.

Example 10

TRACK 80
:26

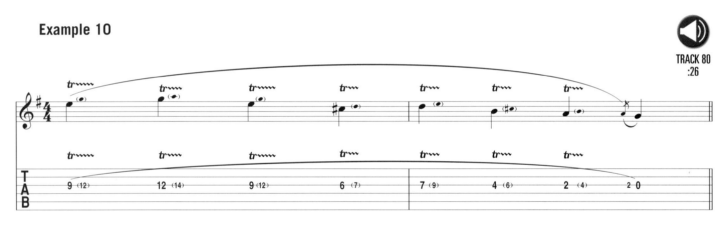

Example 11 is based off a Randy Rhoads lick and is great for building excitement. We travel through a few non-diatonic (out of key) notes on the way up.

Example 11

TRACK 81
:00

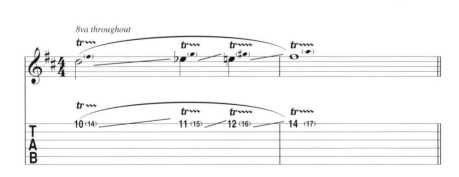

Here's another fun trick with the tapped trill. We maintain the same tapped note, but move our fret-hand down so the trill gets wider and wider. You can also get the opposite effect by maintaining the pitch of the fret hand and moving the tapped trill note. Or, you can get a similar effect, as Steve Vai does in "Tender Surrender," by trilling against an open string and moving the fret-hand note. On the audio, I'm tapping with the pick, but feel free to try it with just your tapping finger as well.

Example 12

TRACK 81
:10

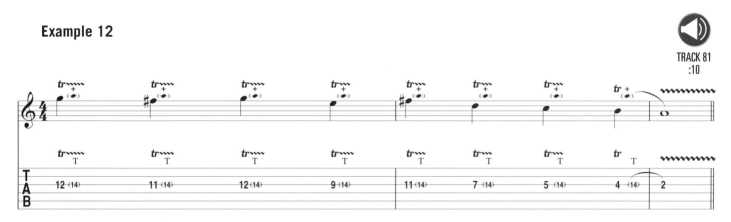

For our final lick, we're moving the tapped alternating trill up through the D minor hexatonic scale on the G string. In this instance, we start each trill with a tap, so the higher note of the trill is sounding first, which is unusual.

Example 13

TRACK 81
:22

* Execute trills by alternating tapping finger and fret-hand finger.

SUGGESTED LISTENING

Jimi Hendrix: "Voodoo Child"

Metallica: "One"

Steve Vai: "Tender Surrender"

Spinal Tap: "Tonight I'm Gonna Rock You Tonight"

Ozzy Osbourne: "Crazy Train"

Joe Satriani: "Surfing with the Alien"

VIBRATO

Vibrato is one of the most expressive devices we have on the guitar, and it's a shame that more players don't spend time cultivating it. There are some players for which it comes naturally, while others have to work at it. It can be learned though, just like any other technique, and it's well worth the effort. It's hard to even imagine the licks of Hendrix, Clapton, Stevie Ray, Steve Vai, or Zakk Wylde without their trademark vibratos. An extension of your personality and attitude, it's one of the most identifiable traits of any guitar player.

Just as with many guitar techniques, there are numerous methods used to produce vibrato. There's no one correct method, and many players actually master several different types. The motion Eric Clapton uses is completely different than what Hendrix used, and both are equally beautiful in sound. We'll look at the two main types of vibrato used in rock here (epitomized by those two mentioned), but feel free to experiment on your own in this regard.

Technical Talk

Vibrato is a fluctuation of pitch. It can be fast, slow, controlled, frenetic, subtle, over-the-top, or any combination thereof. On the electric guitar, vibrato is usually created by slightly bending a string and releasing it to its unbent state over and over. Because of this, vibrato on a standard fretted note will always alternate between in tune and slightly sharp; this results in an "average" note that's actually slightly out of tune. (Adding vibrato to bent notes is another story. We'll look at that in a bit.)

The more drastic the bend, the "wider" the vibrato sounds. This is why Zakk Wylde's vibrato sounds different than Eric Clatpon's. Again, there's no one correct way here. Different types of vibrato will suit different styles of music more appropriately than others. A huge, exaggerated vibrato would tend to sound out of place on a tender ballad, whereas a graceful, subtle vibrato would hardly be noticed in a hard rock tune.

Hendrix Style – Wrist Motion

The Hendrix style of vibrato is perhaps what most consider to be the classic rock vibrato. It's most commonly used with the first finger, though it can be used with any. The motion comes from rotating the wrist back and forth, similar to the act of turning a door knob. It'll take a while to get the fluidity down, but once you do, it's a very musical vibrato. You should practice slowly at first and build up the speed gradually. Be sure to practice with every finger as well, because it's nice to be able to add vibrato on any note.

You'll notice that, on string 1, you'll need to modify the motion a bit, or you'll fall off the edge of the frets. Whereas on all the other strings, most players pull down (toward the floor) for the slight bends during the vibrato, on string 1, you'll need to push up (toward the ceiling).

Wrist vibrato on string 1

Clapton Style – Forearm Motion

The other most popular school of vibrato is the Clapton variety, where the motion comes from the forearm. With this type, the wrist remains in place, but the entire hand is pushed up and down with the forearm. Generally, most players tend to bend and release up toward the ceiling when using this style, which is opposite from the wrist type. This means that, of course, you'll need to make an adjustment on string 6 so you don't push the string off the edge.

Honorable Mentions

There are several other types of vibrato used that aren't as common but still worthy of mention. Here's a brief description of them.

- **Lateral/Classical**: This is a very subtle vibrato used mostly by classical guitarists and some jazz players, although you do find the occasional rock guitarist employing it. It's created by tugging on the string back and forth along the length of the string—not perpendicular to the neck. It's easiest to create when you're in the middle of the string (i.e., around fret 12). Also interesting is the fact that the pitch falls flat (when pushing toward the bridge) and rises sharp (when pulling toward the nut), thus causing the average note to be "in tune."

- **Finger Vibrato**: This vibrato is generated by simply wiggling the finger joints themselves; the wrist and forearm are kept stationary. This also tends to be a bit more subtle.

- **Circular**: This is kind of a combination of the wrist style and the lateral style. It's a bit hard to describe, but it's very musical once achieved. A major proponent of this vibrato is Steve Vai, who uses it quite frequently.

Adding Vibrato to Bent Notes

It's quite common in rock to add vibrato to bent notes as well. The basic idea is to bend to pitch and slightly release over and over again. In this case, you have the ability to generate an average note that's in tune, because you can control exactly where the pitch peaks in each direction. Vibrato on bent notes is most commonly applied with the third finger while pushing the string up toward the ceiling, but it can be applied to any finger with a bend in either direction.

Licks

Ok, let's hear how vibrato can dress up some licks. This first lick in B minor uses the wrist type vibrato on the most common note in this regard: the minor 3rd of a minor pentatonic scale on string 3. You've heard this in literally thousands of solos. We also finish off by applying vibrato with the third finger.

Example 1

TRACK 82
:00

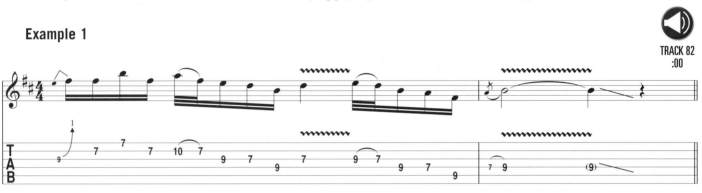

This lick in A takes place in the B.B. box and is reminiscent of Clapton. We're using the forearm vibrato here with the first and third fingers.

Example 2

TRACK 82
:11

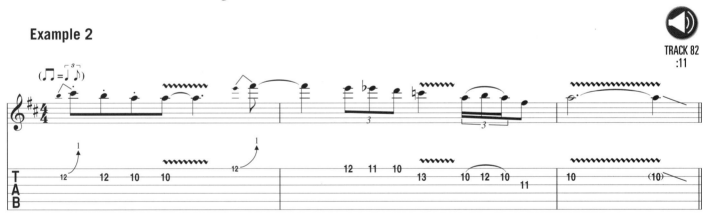

In this Hendrix/Stevie Ray-type example, we're applying wrist vibrato to two strings simultaneously, which will take a bit of getting used to. The motion is the same, but you'll need to probably shift the pressure of your fretting finger slightly so that both notes sound out clearly.

Example 3

TRACK 83
:00

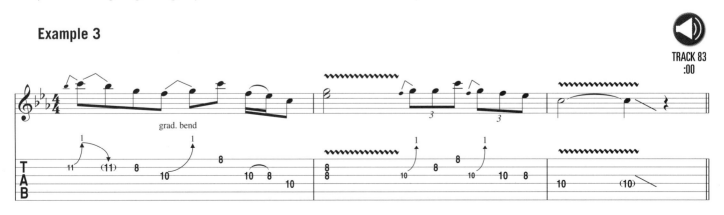

Here's a D minor lick where we're applying vibrato to a note on string 2 that's bent up a whole step to the tonic. This is another hugely common application.

Example 4

TRACK 83
:10

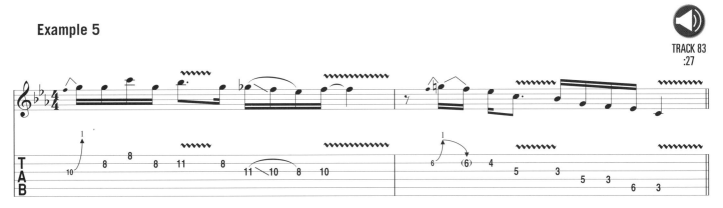

In this final example, we're applying wrist vibrato with every finger on the fret hand. Aren't you glad you practiced it with every finger?

Example 5

TRACK 83
:27

SUGGESTED LISTENING

Jimi Hendrix: "Voodoo Child," "Red House"

Cream: "Spoonful," "Crossroads"

Steve Vai: "For the Love of God," "Tender Surrender"

Stevie Ray Vaughan: "Tightrope"

Ozzy Osborune: "Crazy Babies"

VOLUME SWELLS

If you haven't messed around with volume swells, you don't know what you're missing. They're incredibly fun, and they can produce some very non-guitar-like sounds. Depending on your approach, you can emulate strings, flutes, or synths with volume swells, or they can make a standard bend *really* cry in the hands of Roy Buchanan or Mark Knopfler.

Technical Talk

Volume swells are usually created by a guitar player one of two ways: with the volume knob on the guitar or with a volume pedal. The basic idea involves picking a note while the volume is off and then raising the volume so the note "swells" into being. The use of ambient effects such as reverb and/or delay is common with the technique, as it adds length to the notes and provides an ethereal vibe.

Volume Knob

When using a volume knob on the guitar, most players prefer a Strat-style guitar, since the volume control can be operated with the pinky while plucking strings with the pick. It'll take a bit of coordination to get this down, but with practice will become second nature.

Alternatively, the knob can be twisted with the pick-hand while the fret hand performs "hammer-ons from nowhere" to sound the notes (see the Legato chapter). This technique is often paired with a delay set to a dotted eighth note. You can play straight eighth notes, and the delayed note falls between the cracks to create a sixteenth-note line. This is the trick Eddie Van Halen used on "Cathedral." You need to be very precise with the fret hand and/or employ some fret-hand muting when using this technique if you want to achieve the clarity Eddie achieves.

Volume Pedal

A volume pedal allows for a bit more flexibility, because you can pick and fret notes normally and still apply swells at will with your foot. When you press the pedal all the way down (toe down), the volume is at full capacity. With the pedal all the way up (heel down), the volume is off completely. If you decide to go with a volume pedal, be sure to go try some out before you buy them, as they are not all created equal. Some pedals have a much smoother envelope to them and/or are much better made, and you generally get what you pay for in this regard.

Licks

Let's check out how these swells can add life to otherwise typical phrases. This first example is simply the notes of an A minor pentatonic scale treated to volume swells. If you were to play this line in a standard fashion, it would sound pretty unremarkable. There's a good bit of reverb and delay added on the audio to enhance the effect.

Example 1

TRACK 84
:00

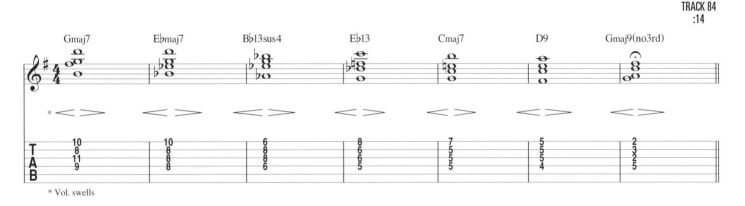

* Vol. swells

Here's a nice sound that's created with a good dose of delay (with lots of feedback) and compression. You play some nice, lush chords and swell into each. It creates a sound closer to a synth pad patch than a guitar.

Example 2

TRACK 84
:14

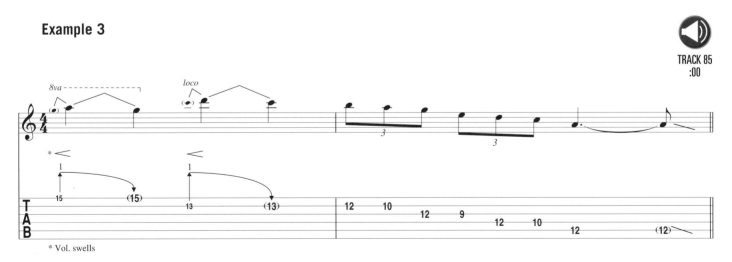

* Vol. swells

This lick is in the vein of Mark Knopfler or Roy Buchanan. The pre-bends begin to release just as the notes swell in, creating a weeping effect. Again, some delay will enhance things.

Example 3

TRACK 85
:00

* Vol. swells

And let's close out with the timed delay trick. We do something similar in the Toggle Switch Stutter Effect chapter as well. We're swelling into straight eighth notes here, and the delayed note falls in between the notes we play to create a sixteenth-note line. For this trick, use a loud delay with only one repeat, and try to keep your swells brief. If you're on a Strat, you can pick each note and swell up with your pinky on the knob. For Gibson-style guitars, you'll probably have to use the "hammer-on from nowhere" technique (see the Legato chapter) and swell the knob with your right hand; alternatively, of course, you can use a volume pedal.

Example 4

TRACK 85
:13

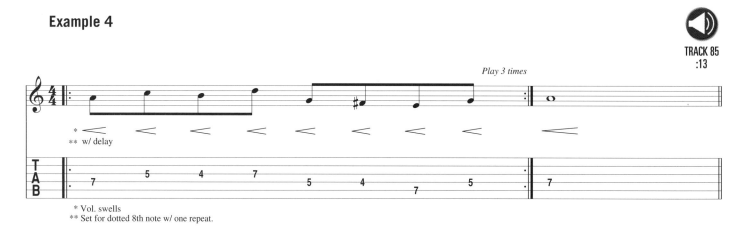

* Vol. swells
** Set for dotted 8th note w/ one repeat.

SUGGESTED LISTENING

Dire Straits: "Brothers in Arms," "You and Your Friend"

Eric Johnson: "East Wes"

Van Halen: "Cathedral," "Panama"

Yngwie Malmsteen: "Black Star"

Fleetwood Mac: "Dreams"

WHAMMY BAR TRICKS

The first successful design of the whammy bar was invented by Paul Bigsby in the forties at the request of the legendary Merle Travis. In fact, Bigsby vibrato systems still grace many guitars today made by Gretsch, Gibson, and others. In the eighties, though, this design got an upgrade with models by Floyd Rose and Kahler, among others. These designs came with locking nuts and also allowed the bar to be pulled back to raise the pitch as well as dip it. Guitarists of that time had a field day with this, and by the middle of the decade, virtually every hard rock guitar was outfitted with one of these units. Eddie Van Halen, Steve Vai, Joe Satriani, Richie Sambora, and countless others abused their whammys in search of strange, funny, and unusual guitar noises. Before you knew it, the bar had left an indelible impact on rock guitar.

Technical Talk

The traditional name for the whammy bar is the *vibrato bar*, because it allows the fluctuation of pitch. (In the fifties, Fender misnamed their version as a tremolo bar while misnaming the tremolo on their amps as vibrato!) The early units such as the Bigsby mainly only allow the pitch to be dropped (though it can be slightly raised on a Bigsby), and they were in fact designed to add vibrato to chords and single notes. The whammys of the eighties through to today can and are still used for that purpose, but they've developed a wackier streak as well. Let's take a look at the main uses for the wiggle bar.

Vibrato

Vibrato is the easiest effect to produce with the bar. Simply sustain a note or chord and gently depress and release the bar repeatedly. The farther you push the bar down, the wider the vibrato will be. It can be anywhere from a subtle ripple to a treacherous avalanche. Try it on chords as well.

Example 1

TRACK 86

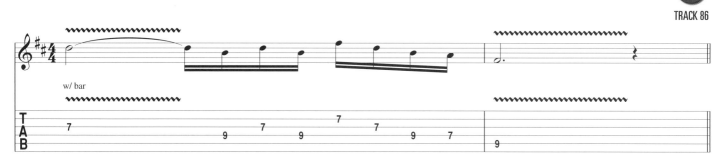

Dip

The dip is a quick drop in pitch followed by a return to normal pitch. It was used a good deal by Chet Atkins, and is equally effective on chords or single notes. It's often done in rhythm, as demonstrated by this example.

Example 2

TRACK 87

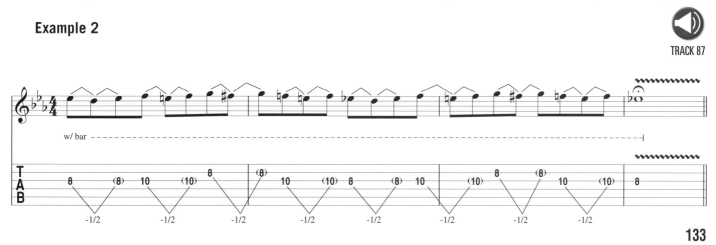

Scoop

To execute a scoop, you dip the bar before the pick the note. As you pick, release the bar back up to pitch. This results in a flat note that quickly rises to pitch. Again, the depth of the scoop is left up to the discretion of the scooper.

Example 3

TRACK 88

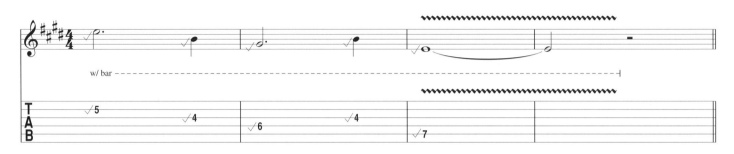

Dive Bomb

This is probably one of the first things many players do when they first get a guitar with a whammy on it. It's simple, but it's just plain fun. Play a note, usually the open low E string, and slowly depress the bar until the strings go slack and stick to the pickups.

Example 4

TRACK 89

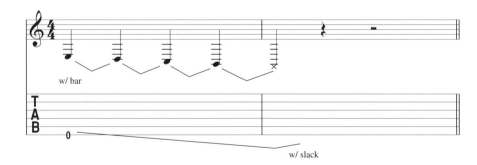

Siren

There are a few different ways to do this. The G string is probably the most commonly used string. The first method is to pick a natural harmonic on the fourth fret or closer to the nut—basically the highest one that you can get to sound clearly. When you get a good scream, pull and push the bar back and forth to imitate a police car siren.The other method, mastered by Joe Satriani, is to play a pinch harmonic on the open G string—you'll have to experiment to find the best place along the string—and then use your fret hand to maneuver the bar. Be sure to pull over to the side to let the ambulance get by clearly; it's the law.

Example 5

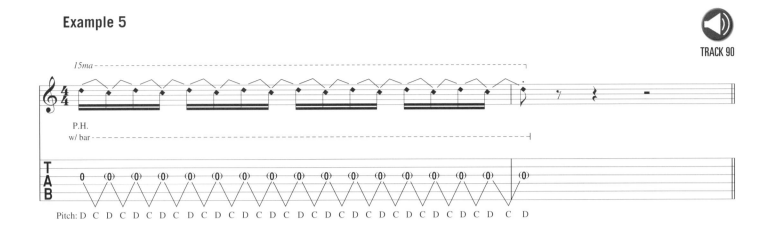

Rubber Band Trill

This trick is another easy one but always a crowd pleaser. While trilling with the fret hand (minor 3rds are common), slowly depress and return the bar. Or you can raise the pitch if your heart desires. Or do both.

Example 6

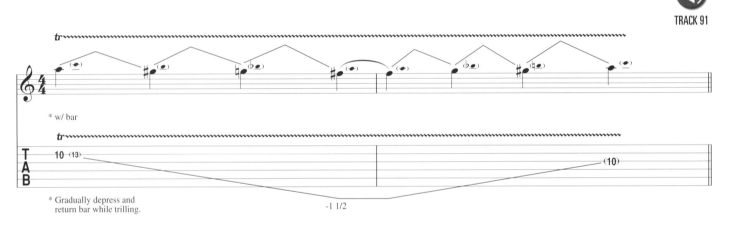

Snake Down the Throat

Ok, so the name's a little provocative. It's an interesting sound, all right? To pull this move off, you pick a note and then begin to slide up the fretboard. As you do this, you depress the whammy bar. The goal is to maintain a steady pitch by slackening the string as you slide up the neck. It's kind of gross sounding, to be honest.

Example 7

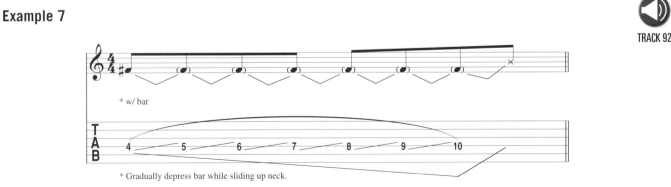

Flutter

This one has Vai written all over it. To execute a flutter, you pick a note and then swat at the end of the bar quickly, as if you were trying to swat a fly. The goal is to depress the bar very quickly and then allow it to snap back into place. It's quite a rude awakening. You can also just use hammer-ons from nowhere in the fret hand and flutter each note from the very beginning.

Example 8

TRACK 93

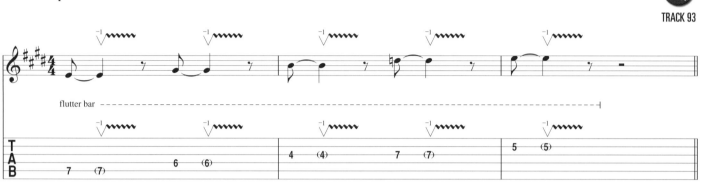

Reverse Scoop (Hiccup)

This next technique goes by various names. Steve Vai calls it "little grace notes from India." The idea here is to turn the bar around so that it's pointing away from the neck. You play notes with your fret hand using all legato techniques. At the beginning of every note, though, you quickly dip the bar. Since it's turned around, this will actually cause the pitch to go sharp, which creates quite an interesting effect.

Example 9

TRACK 94

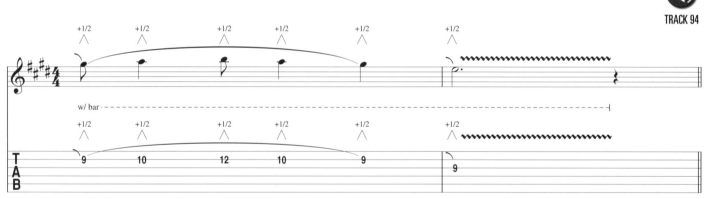

The Elephant

Last but by no means least, we have the elephant. You will impress many a friend with this one at parties. Begin with your volume rolled off. Play the natural harmonics notated in the music; be sure to really whack them and let them all ring together. Then, lower the bar a bit with the pick hand. As you begin to raise the bar, start to swell the volume knob up with your fret hand. Bring the bar up past normal pitch and smoothly dive it down once again. You're on a safari!

Example 10

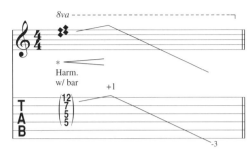

*Vol. swell into harmonics while manipulating bar.

SUGGESTED LISTENING

Joe Satriani: "Satch Boogie," "Surfing with the Alien"

Steve Vai: "Big Trouble" (with David Lee Roth), "The Animal," "Blue Powder"

Van Halen: "Eruption," "Summer Nights"

Jeff Beck: "Where Were You"

GUITAR NOTATION LEGEND

Guitar Music can be notated three different ways: on a *musical staff*, in *tablature*, and in *rhythm slashes*.

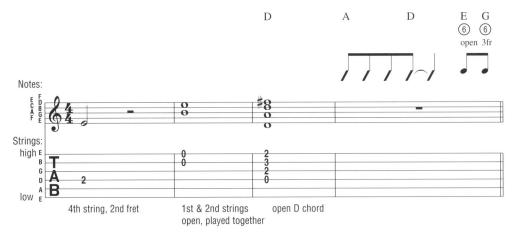

RHYTHM SLASHES are written above the staff. Strum chords in the rhythm indicated. Use the chord diagrams found at the top of the first page of the transcription for the appropriate chord voicings. Round noteheads indicate single notes.

THE MUSICAL STAFF shows pitches and rhythms and is divided by bar lines into measures. Pitches are named after the first seven letters of the alphabet.

TABLATURE graphically represents the guitar fingerboard. Each horizontal line represents a a string, and each number represents a fret.

4th string, 2nd fret

1st & 2nd strings open, played together

open D chord

DEFINITIONS FOR SPECIAL GUITAR NOTATION

HALF-STEP BEND: Strike the note and bend up 1/2 step.

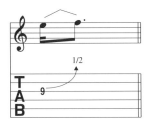

WHOLE-STEP BEND: Strike the note and bend up one step.

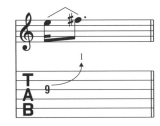

GRACE NOTE BEND: Strike the note and immediately bend up as indicated.

SLIGHT (MICROTONE) BEND: Strike the note and bend up 1/4 step.

BEND AND RELEASE: Strike the note and bend up as indicated, then release back to the original note. Only the first note is struck.

PRE-BEND: Bend the note as indicated, then strike it.

PRE-BEND AND RELEASE: Bend the note as indicated. Strike it and release the bend back to the original note.

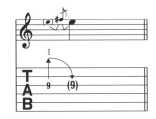

UNISON BEND: Strike the two notes simultaneously and bend the lower note up to the pitch of the higher.

VIBRATO: The string is vibrated by rapidly bending and releasing the note with the fretting hand.

WIDE VIBRATO: The pitch is varied to a greater degree by vibrating with the fretting hand.

HAMMER-ON: Strike the first (lower) note with one finger, then sound the higher note (on the same string) with another finger by fretting it without picking.

PULL-OFF: Place both fingers on the notes to be sounded. Strike the first note and without picking, pull the finger off to sound the second (lower) note.

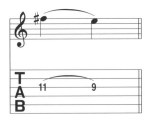

LEGATO SLIDE: Strike the first note and then slide the same fret-hand finger up or down to the second note. The second note is not struck.

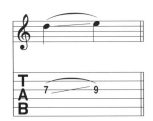

SHIFT SLIDE: Same as legato slide, except the second note is struck.

TRILL: Very rapidly alternate between the notes indicated by continuously hammering on and pulling off.

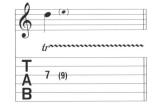

TAPPING: Hammer ("tap") the fret indicated with the pick-hand index or middle finger and pull off to the note fretted by the fret hand.

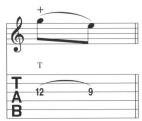

138

NATURAL HARMONIC: Strike the note while the fret-hand lightly touches the string directly over the fret indicated.

PINCH HARMONIC: The note is fretted normally and a harmonic is produced by adding the edge of the thumb or the tip of the index finger of the pick hand to the normal pick attack.

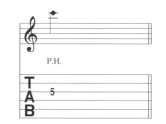

HARP HARMONIC: The note is fretted normally and a harmonic is produced by gently resting the pick hand's index finger directly above the indicated fret (in parentheses) while the pick hand's thumb or pick assists by plucking the appropriate string.

PICK SCRAPE: The edge of the pick is rubbed down (or up) the string, producing a scratchy sound.

MUFFLED STRINGS: A percussive sound is produced by laying the fret hand across the string(s) without depressing, and striking them with the pick hand.

PALM MUTING: The note is partially muted by the pick hand lightly touching the string(s) just before the bridge.

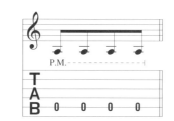

RAKE: Drag the pick across the strings indicated with a single motion.

TREMOLO PICKING: The note is picked as rapidly and continuously as possible.

ARPEGGIATE: Play the notes of the chord indicated by quickly rolling them from bottom to top.

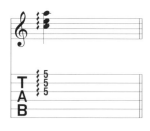

VIBRATO BAR DIVE AND RETURN: The pitch of the note or chord is dropped a specified number of steps (in rhythm) then returned to the original pitch.

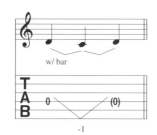

VIBRATO BAR SCOOP: Depress the bar just before striking the note, then quickly release the bar.

VIBRATO BAR DIP: Strike the note and the immediately drop a specified number of steps, then release back to the original pitch.

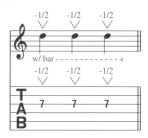

ADDITIONAL MUSICAL DEFINITIONS

(accent)	•	Accentuate note (play it louder)
(accent)	•	Accentuate note with great intensity
(staccato)	•	Play the note short
⊓	•	Downstroke
∨	•	Upstroke
D.S. al Coda	•	Go back to the sign (𝄋), then play until the measure marked "**To Coda**," then skip to the section labelled "**Coda**."
D.C. al Fine	•	Go back to the beginning of the song and play until the measure marked "**Fine**" (end).

Rhy. Fig.	•	Label used to recall a recurring accompaniment pattern (usually chordal).
Riff	•	Label used to recall composed, melodic lines (usually single notes) which recur.
Fill	•	Label used to identify a brief melodic figure which is to be inserted into the arrangement.
Rhy. Fill	•	A chordal version of a Fill.
tacet	•	Instrument is silent (drops out).
	•	Repeat measures between signs.
1. 2.	•	When a repeated section has different endings, play the first ending only the first time and the second ending only the second time.

NOTE: Tablature numbers in parentheses mean:
1. The note is being sustained over a system (note in standard notation is tied), or
2. The note is sustained, but a new articulation (such as a hammer-on, pull-off, slide or vibrato begins), or
3. The note is a barely audible "ghost" note (note in standard notation is also in parentheses).

GUITAR RECORDED VERSIONS®

Guitar Recorded Versions® are note-for-note transcriptions of guitar music taken directly off recordings. This series, one of the most popular in print today, features some of the greatest guitar players and groups from blues and rock to country and jazz.

Guitar Recorded Versions are transcribed by the best transcribers in the business. Every book contains notes and tablature. Visit www.halleonard.com for our complete selection.

AUTHENTIC TRANSCRIPTIONS WITH NOTES AND TABLATURE

00690959	John 5 – Requiem	$22.95
00690814	John 5 – Songs for Sanity	$19.95
00690751	John 5 – Vertigo	$19.95
00694912	Eric Johnson – Ah Via Musicom	$19.95
00690660	Best of Eric Johnson	$22.99
00690845	Eric Johnson – Bloom	$19.95
00691076	Eric Johnson – Up Close	$22.99
00690169	Eric Johnson – Venus Isle	$22.95
00690846	Jack Johnson and Friends – Sing-A-Longs and Lullabies for the Film Curious George	$19.95
00690271	Robert Johnson – The New Transcriptions	$24.95
00699131	Best of Janis Joplin	$19.95
00690427	Best of Judas Priest	$22.99
00690651	Juanes – Exitos de Juanes	$19.95
00690277	Best of Kansas	$19.95
00690911	Best of Phil Keaggy	$24.99
00690727	Toby Keith Guitar Collection	$19.99
00690888	The Killers – Sam's Town	$19.95
00690504	Very Best of Albert King	$19.95
00690444	B.B. King & Eric Clapton – Riding with the King	$22.99
00690134	Freddie King Collection	$19.95
00691062	Kings of Leon – Come Around Sundown	$22.99
00690975	Kings of Leon – Only by the Night	$22.99
00690339	Best of the Kinks	$19.95
00690157	Kiss – Alive!	$19.95
00690356	Kiss – Alive II	$22.99
00694903	Best of Kiss for Guitar	$24.95
00690355	Kiss – Destroyer	$16.95
14026320	Mark Knopfler – Get Lucky	$22.99
00690164	Mark Knopfler Guitar – Vol. 1	$19.95
00690163	Mark Knopfler/Chet Atkins – Neck and Neck	$19.95
00690780	Korn – Greatest Hits, Volume 1	$22.95
00690836	Korn – See You on the Other Side	$19.95
00690377	Kris Kristofferson Collection	$19.95
00690861	Kutless – Hearts of the Innocent	$19.95
00690834	Lamb of God – Ashes of the Wake	$19.95
00690875	Lamb of God – Sacrament	$19.95
00690977	Ray LaMontagne – Gossip in the Grain	$19.99
00690890	Ray LaMontagne – Till the Sun Turns Black	$19.95
00690823	Ray LaMontagne – Trouble	$19.95
00691057	Ray LaMontagne and the Pariah Dogs – God Willin' & The Creek Don't Rise	$22.99
00690658	Johnny Lang – Long Time Coming	$19.95
00690679	John Lennon – Guitar Collection	$19.95
00690781	Linkin Park – Hybrid Theory	$22.95
00690782	Linkin Park – Meteora	$22.95
00690922	Linkin Park – Minutes to Midnight	$19.95
00690783	Best of Live	$19.95
00699623	The Best of Chuck Loeb	$19.95
00690743	Los Lonely Boys	$19.95
00690720	Lostprophets – Start Something	$19.95
00690525	Best of George Lynch	$24.99
00690955	Lynyrd Skynyrd – All-Time Greatest Hits	$19.99
00694954	New Best of Lynyrd Skynyrd	$19.95
00690577	Yngwie Malmsteen – Anthology	$24.95
00694845	Yngwie Malmsteen – Fire and Ice	$19.95
00694757	Yngwie Malmsteen – Trilogy	$19.95
00690754	Marilyn Manson – Lest We Forget	$19.95
00694956	Bob Marley – Legend	$19.95
00690548	Very Best of Bob Marley & The Wailers – One Love	$22.99
00694945	Bob Marley – Songs of Freedom	$24.95
00690914	Maroon 5 – It Won't Be Soon Before Long	$19.95
00690657	Maroon 5 – Songs About Jane	$19.95
00690748	Maroon 5 – 1.22.03 Acoustic	$19.95
00690989	Mastodon – Crack the Skye	$22.99
00691176	Mastodon – The Hunter	$22.99
00690442	Matchbox 20 – Mad Season	$19.95
00690616	Matchbox Twenty – More Than You Think You Are	$19.95
00690239	Matchbox 20 – Yourself or Someone like You	$19.95
00691034	Andy McKee – Joyland	$19.99
00690382	Sarah McLachlan – Mirrorball	$19.95
00120080	The Don McLean Songbook	$19.95
00694952	Megadeth – Countdown to Extinction	$22.95
00690244	Megadeth – Cryptic Writings	$19.95
00694951	Megadeth – Rust in Peace	$22.95
00690011	Megadeth – Youthanasia	$19.95
00690505	John Mellencamp Guitar Collection	$19.95
00690562	Pat Metheny – Bright Size Life	$19.95
00691073	Pat Metheny with Christian McBride & Antonion Sanchez – Day Trip/Tokyo Day Trip Live	$22.99
00690646	Pat Metheny – One Quiet Night	$19.95
00690559	Pat Metheny – Question & Answer	$19.95
00690040	Steve Miller Band Greatest Hits	$19.95
00690769	Modest Mouse – Good News for People Who Love Bad News	$19.95
00694802	Gary Moore – Still Got the Blues	$22.99
00691005	Best of Motion City Soundtrack	$19.99
00690787	Mudvayne – L.D. 50	$22.95
00691070	Mumford & Sons – Sigh No More	$22.99
00690996	My Morning Jacket Collection	$19.99
00690984	Matt Nathanson – Some Mad Hope	$22.99
00690611	Nirvana	$22.95
00694895	Nirvana – Bleach	$19.95
00690189	Nirvana – From the Muddy Banks of the Wishkah	$19.95
00694913	Nirvana – In Utero	$19.95
00694883	Nirvana – Nevermind	$19.95
00690026	Nirvana – Unplugged in New York	$19.95
00120112	No Doubt – Tragic Kingdom	$22.95
00690226	Oasis – The Other Side of Oasis	$19.95
00307163	Oasis – Time Flies... 1994-2009	$19.99
00690358	The Offspring – Americana	$19.95
00690203	The Offspring – Smash	$18.95
00690818	The Best of Opeth	$22.95
00691052	Roy Orbison – Black & White Night	$22.99
00694847	Best of Ozzy Osbourne	$22.95
00690399	Ozzy Osbourne – The Ozzman Cometh	$22.99
00690129	Ozzy Osbourne – Ozzmosis	$22.95
00690933	Best of Brad Paisley	$22.95
00690995	Brad Paisley – Play: The Guitar Album	$24.99
00690866	Panic! At the Disco – A Fever You Can't Sweat Out	$19.95
00690939	Christopher Parkening – Solo Pieces	$19.99
00690594	Best of Les Paul	$19.95
00694855	Pearl Jam – Ten	$22.99
00690439	A Perfect Circle – Mer De Noms	$19.95
00690661	A Perfect Circle – Thirteenth Step	$19.95
00690725	Best of Carl Perkins	$19.99
00690499	Tom Petty – Definitive Guitar Collection	$19.95
00690868	Tom Petty – Highway Companion	$19.95
00690176	Phish – Billy Breathes	$22.95
00690428	Pink Floyd – Dark Side of the Moon	$19.95
00690789	Best of Poison	$19.95
00693864	Best of The Police	$19.95
00690299	Best of Elvis: The King of Rock 'n' Roll	$19.95
00692535	Elvis Presley	$19.95
00690925	The Very Best of Prince	$22.99
00690003	Classic Queen	$24.95
00694975	Queen – Greatest Hits	$24.95
00690670	Very Best of Queensryche	$19.95
00690878	The Raconteurs – Broken Boy Soldiers	$19.95
00694910	Rage Against the Machine	$19.95
00690179	Rancid – And Out Come the Wolves	$22.95
00690426	Best of Ratt	$19.95
00690055	Red Hot Chili Peppers – Blood Sugar Sex Magik	$19.95
00690584	Red Hot Chili Peppers – By the Way	$19.95
00690379	Red Hot Chili Peppers – Californication	$19.95
00690673	Red Hot Chili Peppers – Greatest Hits	$19.95
00690090	Red Hot Chili Peppers – One Hot Minute	$22.95
00691166	Red Hot Chili Peppers – I'm with You	$22.99
00690852	Red Hot Chili Peppers – Stadium Arcadium	$24.95
00690893	The Red Jumpsuit Apparatus – Don't You Fake It	$19.95
00690511	Django Reinhardt – The Definitive Collection	$19.95
00690779	Relient K – MMHMM	$19.95
00690643	Relient K – Two Lefts Don't Make a Right ... But Three Do	$19.95
00690260	Jimmie Rodgers Guitar Collection	$19.95
00690014	Rolling Stones – Exile on Main Street	$24.95
00690631	Rolling Stones – Guitar Anthology	$27.95
00690685	David Lee Roth – Eat 'Em and Smile	$19.95
00690031	Santana's Greatest Hits	$19.95
00690796	Very Best of Michael Schenker	$19.95
00690566	Best of Scorpions	$22.95
00690604	Bob Seger – Guitar Anthology	$19.95
00690659	Bob Seger and the Silver Bullet Band – Greatest Hits, Volume 2	$17.95
00691012	Shadows Fall – Retribution	$22.99
00690896	Shadows Fall – Threads of Life	$19.95
00690803	Best of Kenny Wayne Shepherd Band	$19.95
00690750	Kenny Wayne Shepherd – The Place You're In	$19.95
00690857	Shinedown – Us and Them	$19.95
00690196	Silverchair – Freak Show	$19.95
00690130	Silverchair – Frogstomp	$19.95
00690872	Slayer – Christ Illusion	$19.95
00690813	Slayer – Guitar Collection	$19.95
00690419	Slipknot	$19.95
00690973	Slipknot – All Hope Is Gone	$22.99
00690733	Slipknot – Volume 3 (The Subliminal Verses)	$22.99
00690330	Social Distortion – Live at the Roxy	$19.95
00120004	Best of Steely Dan	$24.95
00694921	Best of Steppenwolf	$22.95
00690655	Best of Mike Stern	$19.95
00690949	Rod Stewart Guitar Anthology	$19.99
00690021	Sting – Fields of Gold	$19.95
00690597	Stone Sour	$19.95
00690689	Story of the Year – Page Avenue	$19.95

RECORDED VERSIONS GUITAR®

AUTHENTIC TRANSCRIPTIONS WITH NOTES AND TABLATURE

00690520	Styx Guitar Collection	$19.95
00120081	Sublime	$19.95
00690992	Sublime – Robbin' the Hood	$19.99
00690519	SUM 41 – All Killer No Filler	$19.95
00691072	Best of Supertramp	$22.99
00690994	Taylor Swift	$22.99
00690993	Taylor Swift – Fearless	$22.99
00691063	Taylor Swift – Speak Now	$22.99
00690767	Switchfoot – The Beautiful Letdown	$19.95
00690830	System of a Down – Hypnotize	$19.95
00690531	System of a Down – Toxicity	$19.95
00694824	Best of James Taylor	$16.95
00694887	Best of Thin Lizzy	$19.95
00690671	Three Days Grace	$19.95
00690871	Three Days Grace – One-X	$19.95
00690891	30 Seconds to Mars – A Beautiful Lie	$19.95
00690030	Toad the Wet Sprocket	$19.95
00690233	The Merle Travis Collection	$19.99
00690683	Robin Trower – Bridge of Sighs	$19.95
00699191	U2 – Best of: 1980-1990	$19.95
00690732	U2 – Best of: 1990-2000	$19.95
00690894	U2 – 18 Singles	$19.95
00690775	U2 – How to Dismantle an Atomic Bomb	$22.95
00690997	U2 – No Line on the Horizon	$19.99
00690039	Steve Vai – Alien Love Secrets	$24.95
00690172	Steve Vai – Fire Garden	$24.95
00660137	Steve Vai – Passion & Warfare	$24.95
00690881	Steve Vai – Real Illusions: Reflections	$24.95
00694904	Steve Vai – Sex and Religion	$24.95
00690392	Steve Vai – The Ultra Zone	$19.95
00690024	Stevie Ray Vaughan – Couldn't Stand the Weather	$19.95
00690370	Stevie Ray Vaughan and Double Trouble – The Real Deal: Greatest Hits Volume 2	$22.95
00690116	Stevie Ray Vaughan – Guitar Collection	$24.95
00660136	Stevie Ray Vaughan – In Step	$19.95
00694879	Stevie Ray Vaughan – In the Beginning	$19.95
00660058	Stevie Ray Vaughan – Lightnin' Blues '83-'87	$24.95
00690036	Stevie Ray Vaughan – Live Alive	$24.95
00694835	Stevie Ray Vaughan – The Sky Is Crying	$22.95
00690025	Stevie Ray Vaughan – Soul to Soul	$19.95
00690015	Stevie Ray Vaughan – Texas Flood	$19.95
00690772	Velvet Revolver – Contraband	$22.95
00690132	The T-Bone Walker Collection	$19.95
00694789	Muddy Waters – Deep Blues	$24.95
00690071	Weezer (The Blue Album)	$19.95
00690516	Weezer (The Green Album)	$19.95
00690286	Weezer – Pinkerton	$19.95
00691046	Weezer – Rarities Edition	$22.99
00690447	Best of the Who	$24.95
00694970	The Who – Definitive Guitar Collection: A-E	$24.95
00694971	The Who – Definitive Guitar Collection F-Li	$24.95
00694972	The Who – Definitive Guitar Collection: Lo-R	$24.95
00694973	The Who – Definitive Guitar Collection: S-Y	$24.95
00690672	Best of Dar Williams	$19.95
00691017	Wolfmother – Cosmic Egg	$22.99
00690319	Stevie Wonder – Some of the Best	$17.95
00690596	Best of the Yardbirds	$19.95
00690844	Yellowcard – Lights and Sounds	$19.95
00690916	The Best of Dwight Yoakam	$19.95
00690904	Neil Young – Harvest	$29.99
00690905	Neil Young – Rust Never Sleeps	$19.99
00690443	Frank Zappa – Hot Rats	$19.95
00690624	Frank Zappa and the Mothers of Invention – One Size Fits All	$22.99
00690623	Frank Zappa – Over-Nite Sensation	$22.99
00690589	ZZ Top – Guitar Anthology	$24.95
00690960	ZZ Top Guitar Classics	$19.99

HAL•LEONARD® CORPORATION

7777 W. Bluemound Rd. P.O. Box 13819 Milwaukee, WI 53213

Complete songlists and more at **www.halleonard.com**

Prices, contents, and availability subject to change without notice.

0412

Get Better at Guitar

...with these Great Guitar Instruction Books from Hal Leonard!

101 GUITAR TIPS
INCLUDES TAB

STUFF ALL THE PROS KNOW AND USE

by Adam St. James

This book contains invaluable guidance on everything from scales and music theory to truss rod adjustments, proper recording studio set-ups, and much more. The book also features snippets of advice from some of the most celebrated guitarists and producers in the music business, including B.B. King, Steve Vai, Joe Satriani, Warren Haynes, Laurence Juber, Pete Anderson, Tom Dowd and others, culled from the author's hundreds of interviews.

00695737 Book/CD Pack...........................$16.95

AMAZING PHRASING
INCLUDES TAB

50 WAYS TO IMPROVE YOUR IMPROVISATIONAL SKILLS

by Tom Kolb

This book/CD pack explores all the main components necessary for crafting well-balanced rhythmic and melodic phrases. It also explains how these phrases are put together to form cohesive solos. Many styles are covered – rock, blues, jazz, fusion, country, Latin, funk and more – and all of the concepts are backed up with musical examples. The companion CD contains 89 demos for listening, and most tracks feature full-band backing.

00695583 Book/CD Pack...........................$19.95

BLUES YOU CAN USE
INCLUDES TAB

by John Ganapes

A comprehensive source designed to help guitarists develop both lead and rhythm playing. Covers: Texas, Delta, R&B, early rock and roll, gospel, blues/rock and more. Includes: 21 complete solos • chord progressions and riffs • turnarounds • moveable scales and more. CD features leads and full band backing.

00695007 Book/CD Pack...........................$19.99

FRETBOARD MASTERY
INCLUDES TAB

by Troy Stetina

Untangle the mysterious regions of the guitar fretboard and unlock your potential. *Fretboard Mastery* familiarizes you with all the shapes you need to know by applying them in real musical examples, thereby reinforcing and reaffirming your newfound knowledge. The result is a much higher level of comprehension and retention.

00695331 Book/CD Pack...........................$19.95

FRETBOARD ROADMAPS – 2ND EDITION

ESSENTIAL GUITAR PATTERNS THAT ALL THE PROS KNOW AND USE

by Fred Sokolow

The updated edition of this bestseller features more songs, updated lessons, and a full audio CD! Learn to play lead and rhythm anywhere on the fretboard, in any key; play a variety of lead guitar styles; play chords and progressions anywhere on the fretboard; expand your chord vocabulary; and learn to think musically – the way the pros do.

00695941 Book/CD Pack........................$14.95

GUITAR AEROBICS
INCLUDES TAB

A 52-WEEK, ONE-LICK-PER-DAY WORKOUT PROGRAM FOR DEVELOPING, IMPROVING & MAINTAINING GUITAR TECHNIQUE

by Troy Nelson

From the former editor of *Guitar One* magazine, here is a daily dose of vitamins to keep your chops fine tuned! Musical styles include rock, blues, jazz, metal, country, and funk. Techniques taught include alternate picking, arpeggios, sweep picking, string skipping, legato, string bending, and rhythm guitar. These exercises will increase speed, and improve dexterity and pick- and fret-hand accuracy. The accompanying CD includes all 365 workout licks plus play-along grooves in every style at eight different metronome settings.

00695946 Book/CD Pack........................$19.99

GUITAR CLUES
INCLUDES TAB

OPERATION PENTATONIC

by Greg Koch

Join renowned guitar master Greg Koch as he clues you in to a wide variety of fun and valuable pentatonic scale applications. Whether you're new to improvising or have been doing it for a while, this book/CD pack will provide loads of delicious licks and tricks that you can use right away, from volume swells and chicken pickin' to intervallic and chordal ideas. The CD includes 65 demo and play-along tracks.

00695827 Book/CD Pack........................$19.95

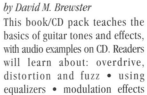

INTRODUCTION TO GUITAR TONE & EFFECTS

by David M. Brewster

This book/CD pack teaches the basics of guitar tones and effects, with audio examples on CD. Readers will learn about: overdrive, distortion and fuzz • using equalizers • modulation effects • reverb and delay • multi-effect processors • and more.

00695766 Book/CD Pack........................$14.95

PICTURE CHORD ENCYCLOPEDIA

This comprehensive guitar chord resource for all playing styles and levels features five voicings of 44 chord qualities for all twelve keys – 2,640 chords in all! For each, there is a clearly illustrated chord frame, as well as *an actual photo* of the chord being played! Includes info on basic fingering principles, open chords and barre chords, partial chords and broken-set forms, and more.

00695224...$19.95

SCALE CHORD RELATIONSHIPS
INCLUDES TAB

by Michael Mueller & Jeff Schroedl

This book teaches players how to determine which scales to play with which chords, so guitarists will never have to fear chord changes again! This book/CD pack explains how to: recognize keys • analyze chord progressions • use the modes • play over nondiatonic harmony • use harmonic and melodic minor scales • use symmetrical scales such as chromatic, whole-tone and diminished scales • incorporate exotic scales such as Hungarian major and Gypsy minor • and much more!

00695563 Book/CD Pack........................$14.95

SPEED MECHANICS FOR LEAD GUITAR
INCLUDES TAB

Take your playing to the stratosphere with the most advanced lead book by this proven heavy metal author. *Speed Mechanics* is the ultimate technique book for developing the kind of speed and precision in today's explosive playing styles. Learn the fastest ways to achieve speed and control, secrets to make your practice time really count, and how to open your ears and make your musical ideas more solid and tangible. Packed with over 200 vicious exercises including Troy's scorching version of "Flight of the Bumblebee." Music and examples demonstrated on CD. 89-minute audio.

00699323 Book/CD Pack........................$19.95

TOTAL ROCK GUITAR
INCLUDES TAB

A COMPLETE GUIDE TO LEARNING ROCK GUITAR

by Troy Stetina

This unique and comprehensive source for learning rock guitar is designed to develop both lead and rhythm playing. It covers: getting a tone that rocks • open chords, power chords and barre chords • riffs, scales and licks • string bending, strumming, palm muting, harmonics and alternate picking • all rock styles • and much more. The examples are in standard notation with chord grids and tab, and the CD includes full-band backing for all 22 songs.

00695246 Book/CD Pack........................$19.99

FOR MORE INFORMATION, SEE YOUR LOCAL MUSIC DEALER, OR WRITE TO:

HAL•LEONARD® CORPORATION
7777 W. BLUEMOUND RD. P.O. BOX 13819 MILWAUKEE, WI 53213

Visit Hal Leonard Online at
www.halleonard.com

Prices, contents, and availability subject to change without notice.

GUITAR *signature licks*

Signature Licks book/CD packs provide a step-by-step breakdown of "right from the record" riffs, licks, and solos so you can jam along with your favorite bands. They contain performance notes and an overview of each artist's or group's style, with note-for-note transcriptions in notes and tab. The CDs feature full-band demos at both normal and slow speeds.

ACOUSTIC CLASSICS
00695864 ....$19.95

AEROSMITH 1973-1979
00695106 ....$22.95

AEROSMITH 1979-1998
00695219 ....$22.95

BEST OF AGGRO-METAL
00695592 ....$19.95

DUANE ALLMAN
00696042 ....$22.99

BEST OF CHET ATKINS
00695752 ....$22.95

AVENGED SEVENFOLD
00696473 ....$22.99

THE BEACH BOYS DEFINITIVE COLLECTION
00695683 ....$22.95

BEST OF THE BEATLES FOR ACOUSTIC GUITAR
00695453 ....$22.95

THE BEATLES BASS
00695283 ....$22.95

THE BEATLES FAVORITES
00695096 ....$24.95

THE BEATLES HITS
00695049 ....$24.95

BEST OF GEORGE BENSON
00695418 ....$22.95

BEST OF BLACK SABBATH
00695249 ....$22.95

BEST OF BLINK - 182
00695704 ....$22.95

BLUES BREAKERS WITH JOHN MAYALL & ERIC CLAPTON
00696374 ....$22.99

BEST OF BLUES GUITAR
00695846 ....$19.95

BLUES/ROCK GUITAR HEROES
00696381 ....$19.99

BLUES/ROCK GUITAR MASTERS
00695348 ....$21.95

KENNY BURRELL
00695830 ....$22.99

BEST OF CHARLIE CHRISTIAN
00695584 ....$22.95

BEST OF ERIC CLAPTON
00695038 ....$24.95

ERIC CLAPTON – THE BLUESMAN
00695040 ....$22.95

ERIC CLAPTON – FROM THE ALBUM UNPLUGGED
00695250 ....$24.95

BEST OF CREAM
00695251 ....$22.95

CREEDANCE CLEARWATER REVIVAL
00695924 ....$22.95

DEEP PURPLE – GREATEST HITS
00695625 ....$22.95

THE BEST OF DEF LEPPARD
00696516 ....$22.95

THE DOORS
00695373 ....$22.95

TOMMY EMMANUEL
00696409 ....$22.99

ESSENTIAL JAZZ GUITAR
00695875 ....$19.99

FAMOUS ROCK GUITAR SOLOS
00695590 ....$19.95

FLEETWOOD MAC
00696416 ....$22.99

ROBBEN FORD
00695903 ....$22.95

GREATEST GUITAR SOLOS OF ALL TIME
00695301 ....$19.95

BEST OF GRANT GREEN
00695747 ....$22.95

BEST OF GUNS N' ROSES
00695183 ....$24.95

THE BEST OF BUDDY GUY
00695186 ....$22.99

JIM HALL
00695848 ....$22.99

HARD ROCK SOLOS
00695591 ....$19.95

JIMI HENDRIX
00696560 ....$24.95

JIMI HENDRIX – VOLUME 2
00695835 ....$24.95

JOHN LEE HOOKER
00695894 ....$19.99

HOT COUNTRY GUITAR
00695580 ....$19.95

BEST OF JAZZ GUITAR
00695586 ....$24.95

ERIC JOHNSON
00699317 ....$24.95

ROBERT JOHNSON
00695264 ....$22.95

BARNEY KESSEL
00696009 ....$22.99

THE ESSENTIAL ALBERT KING
00695713 ....$22.95

B.B. KING – BLUES LEGEND
00696039 ....$22.99

B.B. KING – THE DEFINITIVE COLLECTION
00695635 ....$22.95

B.B. KING – MASTER BLUESMAN
00699923 ....$24.99

THE KINKS
00695553 ....$22.95

BEST OF KISS
00699413 ....$22.95

MARK KNOPFLER
00695178 ....$22.95

LYNYRD SKYNYRD
00695872 ....$24.95

BEST OF PAT MARTINO
00695632 ....$24.99

WES MONTGOMERY
00695387 ....$24.95

BEST OF NIRVANA
00695483 ....$24.95

THE OFFSPRING
00695852 ....$24.95

VERY BEST OF OZZY OSBOURNE
00695431 ....$22.95

BRAD PAISLEY
00696379 ....$22.99

BEST OF JOE PASS
00695730 ....$22.95

JACO PASTORIUS
00695544 ....$24.95

TOM PETTY
00696021 ....$22.99

PINK FLOYD – EARLY CLASSICS
00695566 ....$22.95

THE POLICE
00695724 ....$22.95

THE GUITARS OF ELVIS
00696507 ....$22.95

BEST OF QUEEN
00695097 ....$24.95

BEST OF RAGE AGAINST THE MACHINE
00695480 ....$24.95

RED HOT CHILI PEPPERS
00695173 ....$22.95

RED HOT CHILI PEPPERS – GREATEST HITS
00695828 ....$24.95

BEST OF DJANGO REINHARDT
00695660 ....$24.95

BEST OF ROCK
00695884 ....$19.95

BEST OF ROCK 'N' ROLL GUITAR
00695559 ....$19.95

BEST OF ROCKABILLY GUITAR
00695785 ....$19.95

THE ROLLING STONES
00695079 ....$24.95

BEST OF DAVID LEE ROTH
00695843 ....$24.95

BEST OF JOE SATRIANI
00695216 ....$22.95

BEST OF SILVERCHAIR
00695488 ....$22.95

THE BEST OF SOUL GUITAR
00695703 ....$19.95

BEST OF SOUTHERN ROCK
00695560 ....$19.95

STEELY DAN
00696015 ....$22.99

MIKE STERN
00695800 ....$24.99

BEST OF SURF GUITAR
00695822 ....$19.95

BEST OF SYSTEM OF A DOWN
00695788 ....$22.95

ROBIN TROWER
00695950 ....$22.95

STEVE VAI
00673247 ....$22.95

STEVE VAI – ALIEN LOVE SECRETS: THE NAKED VAMPS
00695223 ....$22.95

STEVE VAI – FIRE GARDEN: THE NAKED VAMPS
00695166 ....$22.95

STEVE VAI – THE ULTRA ZONE: NAKED VAMPS
00695684 ....$22.95

STEVIE RAY VAUGHAN – 2ND ED.
00699316 ....$24.95

THE GUITAR STYLE OF STEVIE RAY VAUGHAN
00695155 ....$24.95

BEST OF THE VENTURES
00695772 ....$19.95

THE WHO – 2ND ED.
00695561 ....$22.95

JOHNNY WINTER
00695951 ....$22.99

BEST OF ZZ TOP
00695738 ....$24.95

HAL•LEONARD®
CORPORATION
7777 W. BLUEMOUND RD. P.O. BOX 13819
MILWAUKEE, WISCONSIN 53213

www.halleonard.com

COMPLETE DESCRIPTIONS AND SONGLISTS ONLINE!
Prices, contents and availability subject to change without notice.

0412

Hal Leonard Guitar Tab White Pages

*These incredible collections contain note-for-note transcriptions
straight from the original recordings. Each edition is over 700 pages!*

GUITAR TAB WHITE PAGES – VOLUME 1 – 2ND EDITION

The primo songlist for this second edition boasts even more of your faves from all styles of music: Aerials • All Apologies • American Woman • Badge • Centerfold • Day Tripper • Dissident • Free Ride • Heartache Tonight • Iron Man • Landslide • Layla • Loser • Misty • My Girl • Name • Oleo • Piece of My Heart • Satin Doll • Signs • Sweet Emotion • Wild Thing • You Shook Me • You Were Meant for Me • more!

00690471 Guitar Recorded Versions $29.99

GUITAR TAB WHITE PAGES – VOLUME 2

Note-for-note guitar tab transcriptions for 150 songs, including: Born Under A Bad Sign • Dancing In The Street • Are You Gonna Go My Way • I Shot The Sheriff • I Want You To Want Me • Little Miss Can't Be Wrong • Runnin' Down A Dream • Welcome To The Jungle • Pride And Joy • Mustang Sally • Freeway Jam • Everyday I Have The Blues • Crazy Train • Jump, Jive An' Wail • Killing Floor • Stayin' Alive • Sweet Talkin' Woman • The Thrill Is Gone • many more!

00699557 Guitar Recorded Versions.................................. $29.99

GUITAR TAB WHITE PAGES – VOLUME 3

By popular demand, here's Volume 3 of our best-selling songbook featuring 150 more great titles: Alive • American Pie • Are You Gonna Be My Girl • Bang a Gong (Get It On) • Carry on Wayward Son • Don't Stand So Close to Me • Fat Lip • Hard to Handle • Jane Says • Jeremy • Killer Queen • Once Bitten Twice Shy • Peg • Santeria • Sweet Home Alabama • What's My Age Again? • Wish You Were Here • Ziggy Stardust • and more.

00690791 Guitar Recorded Versions.................................. $29.99

ACOUSTIC GUITAR TAB WHITE PAGES

150 acoustic favorites from yesterday and today: Across the Universe • At Seventeen • The Boxer • Come to My Window • Crazy on You • Here Comes the Sun • Layla • Learning to Fly • Loser • Maggie May • Mr. Jones • Not Fade Away • Patience • Pink Houses • Suite: Judy Blue Eyes • Superman (It's Not Easy) • Tears in Heaven • Time for Me to Fly • Time in a Bottle • Yellow • You've Got a Friend • and many more unplugged gems.

00699590 Guitar Recorded Versions.................................. $29.99

BLUES GUITAR TAB WHITE PAGES

Blues classics include: Baby, Please Don't Go • Born Under a Bad Sign • Bridge of Sighs • Cold Shot • Couldn't Stand the Weather • Cross Road Blues (Crossroads) • Double Trouble • Everyday I Have the Blues • I Can't Quit You Baby • Killing Floor • Love in Vain Blues • Pride and Joy • The Sky Is Crying • Sweet Home Chicago • Texas Flood • The Thrill Is Gone • and dozens more!

00700131 Guitar Recorded Versions.................................. $29.99

CHRISTIAN GUITAR TAB WHITE PAGES

125+ favorites by today's top CCM artists: Be My Escape • Big House • Bliss • Dare You to Move • Deeper • Engage • Fireproof • Every Little Thing • Flood • Get Down • Hands and Feet • He Reigns • His Eyes • Holy One • I Can Feel It • Into Jesus • Jesus Freak • Jonah • Lifesong • Man of God • My Refuge • Shine • Undo Me • We Are One Tonight • Who I Am Hates Who I've Been • Youth of the Nation • and more.

00690847 Guitar Recorded Versions........................$29.95

EASY GUITAR TAB WHITE PAGES

This awesome songbook packs in over 200 easy arrangements in notes and tab of some of the best guitar songs ever, from all styles of music. Songs include: Ain't Too Proud to Beg • Are You Gonna Be My Girl • Bad Case of Loving You • Bésame Mucho • Crying • Don't Stop • Footloose • Guitars, Cadillacs • Help Me Rhonda • Let's Stay Together • Longer • Me and Bobby McGee • Name • On Broadway • Summer in the City • Three Little Birds • Time Is on My Side • Woman • Zombie • and hundreds more.

00702280 Guitar Recorded Versions $29.99

GUITAR TAB WHITE PAGES PLAY-ALONG

This awesome package contains tab transcriptions of 100 of the greatest rock songs ever, along with six CDs of high-quality, full-band backing tracks that coordinate with the transcriptions. Songs include: All Right Now • Barracuda • Black Hole Sun • Changes • Cheap Sunglasses • Highway to Hell • London Calling • Mony, Mony • Rhiannon • Sultans of Swing • Wish You Were Here • Ziggy Stardust • and scores more.

00701764 Book/6-CD Pack.. $39.99

ALSO AVAILABLE:

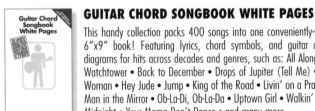

GUITAR CHORD SONGBOOK WHITE PAGES

This handy collection packs 400 songs into one conveniently-sized 6"x9" book! Featuring lyrics, chord symbols, and guitar chord diagrams for hits across decades and genres, such as: All Along the Watchtower • Back to December • Drops of Jupiter (Tell Me) • Evil Woman • Hey Jude • Jump • King of the Road • Livin' on a Prayer • Man in the Mirror • Ob-La-Di, Ob-La-Da • Uptown Girl • Walkin' After Midnight • Your Mama Don't Dance • and many more.

00702609 Lyrics/Chord Symbols/Guitar Chord Diagrams $29.99

Prices, contents, and availability subject to change without notice.

HAL•LEONARD® CORPORATION

7777 W. Bluemound Rd. P.O. Box 13819 Milwaukee, WI 53213

www.halleonard.com

0412